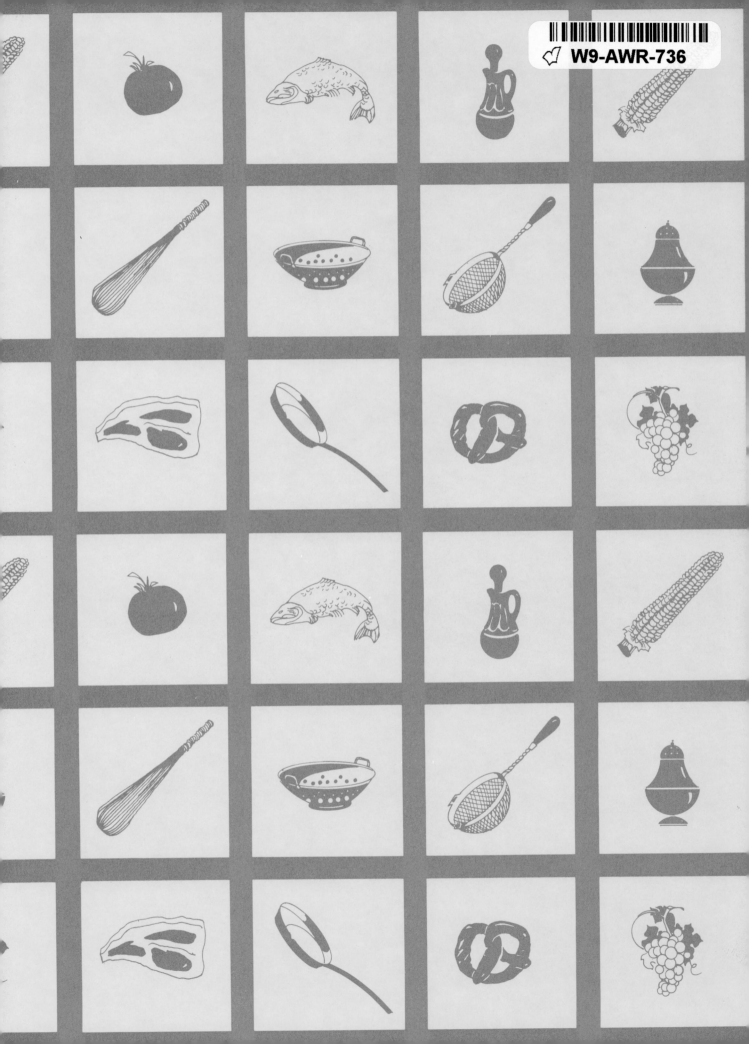

ILLUSTRATED LIBRARY OF COOKING

Cover photo: The famed Smithfield ham of Virginia could be used for the recipes on pages 66 or 69.

TIME LIFE BOOKS

ILLUSTRATED LIBRARY OF COOKING

Lamb & Pork

Culinary Arts Institute®
A DIVISION OF DELAIR PUBLISHING COMPANY

Published, under agreement with Time-Life Books, by
Culinary Arts Institute
a division of
Delair Publishing Company, Inc.
420 Lexington Avenue
New York, New York 10170

These recipes were previously published in a
different format by Time-Life Books.

The Time-Life Illustrated Library of Cooking
is a collection of tested recipes
by leading authorities in the world of cooking.
This volume contains recipes
by the experts listed below:

Michael Field, the consulting editor
for the Foods of the World series,
was one of America's top-ranking cooking experts
and a contributor to leading magazines.

James A. Beard, a renowned authority
on American cuisine, is also
an accomplished teacher and writer
of the culinary arts.

Allison Williams is the author
of *The Embassy Cookbook,*
her collection of authentic recipes
from various embassies in Washington.

ISBN: 0-8326-0805-X

Contents

Lamb

Roast Leg of Lamb

Gigot d' Agneau Rôti   *To serve 6 to 8*

A 5- to 6-pound leg of lamb trimmed of excess fat but with the fell (or parchmentlike covering) left on
1 garlic clove, cut in slivers
3 tablespoons vegetable oil
2 tablespoons salt
2 onions, thinly sliced
2 carrots, thinly sliced
1½ cups fresh or canned beef or chicken stock
½ teaspoon lemon juice
Salt
Freshly ground black pepper

1. Preheat the oven to 500°.
2. Make 6 or 8 quarter-inch incisions on the fatty side of the lamb, and insert a sliver of garlic in each cut.
3. Brush the leg with oil and pat salt all over it.
4. Insert a meat thermometer into the thickest part of the leg, being careful not to touch a bone.
5. Place the leg, fat side up, on a rack in a shallow roasting pan and roast it uncovered for 20 minutes on the middle shelf of the oven.
6. Then reduce the heat to 375°, scatter the vegetables around the rack and roast the lamb for another 40 to 60 minutes, or until done to your liking.
7. For rare lamb, roast it until the meat thermometer reads 130° to 140°; for medium, 140° to 150°; for well done, 150° to 160°.
8. Transfer the lamb to a heated platter and remove the thermometer; let it rest 10 minutes before carving.
9. Meanwhile, skim off the fat from the roasting pan, add the stock to the vegetables and boil briskly on top of the stove for 4 or 5 minutes, scraping in any browned bits clinging to the pan.
10. When the sauce has reached the intensity of flavor desired, strain it through a fine sieve into a saucepan, pressing down hard on the vegetables before discarding them.
11. Skim the sauce of its surface fat; taste the sauce and season it with lemon juice, salt and pepper.
12. Reheat the sauce and serve it with the lamb.

Roast Leg of Lamb with Coffee

Lammstek *To serve 10*

A 5-pound leg of lamb
1 tablespoon salt
½ teaspoon white pepper
2 sliced carrots
2 sliced onions
2 cups beef stock
1 cup strong-brewed coffee
¼ cup heavy cream
½ teaspoon sugar
3 tablespoons flour

1. Preheat the oven to 450°.
2. Trim, rinse and dry the lamb; rub it with the salt and pepper.
3. Place the lamb in a roasting pan and roast in the oven for 20 minutes, turning the leg to brown all sides.
4. Pour off the fat.
5. Add the carrots, onions and 1 cup of the stock.
6. Reduce the oven heat to 350° and roast for 45 minutes, basting occasionally.
7. Mix the coffee, cream and sugar and pour it over the lamb.
8. Roast for 45 minutes longer, basting occasionally.
9. Transfer the lamb to a heated platter.
10. Strain the pan juices and skim the fat.
11. Mix the flour with a little of the remaining stock and stir into the pan juices, cooking and stirring over low heat until the mixture boils.
12. Add the remaining stock and cook 5 minutes longer.
13. Taste for seasoning.
14. Serve the gravy separately in a sauceboat.

Roast Leg of Lamb with Orzo

Giouvetsi *To serve 8*

A 6½- to 7-pound leg of lamb, trimmed of
excess fat but with the fell (the parch-
mentlike covering) left on
1 large garlic clove, peeled and cut
lengthwise into 8 thin slivers
1 teaspoon oregano, crumbled
2 teaspoons salt
Freshly ground black pepper
6 tablespoons fresh lemon juice
2 medium-sized onions, peeled and thinly
sliced
1 cup boiling water
2 cups (about 1 pound) *orzo* **(rice-shaped**
pasta)
½ cup canned tomato purée
Freshly grated *kefalotiri* **or imported**
Parmesan cheese

1. Preheat the oven to 450°.
2. With the tip of a small, sharp knife, make 8 quarter-inch-deep incisions on the fat side of the lamb and insert a sliver of garlic in each.
3. Combine the oregano, 1 teaspoon of the salt, and a few grindings of pepper and press the mixture firmly all over the surface of the lamb.
4. For the most predictable results, insert a meat thermometer into the thickest part of the leg, being careful not to let the tip touch any fat or bone.
5. Place the leg, fat side up, on a rack in a shallow roasting pan and roast it uncovered in the middle of the oven for 20 minutes.
6. Reduce the heat to 350°, baste the leg with a tablespoon or so of lemon juice, and scatter the onions in the bottom of the pan.

Greek style roast leg of lamb is pungent with garlic and oregano. It is served here with *orzo*, a delicious rice-shaped pasta at its best sprinkled with cheese.

7. Roast for 15 minutes more, then baste the lamb again with another tablespoon of lemon juice and pour the cup of boiling water over the onions.

8. Basting periodically with the remaining lemon juice, continue roasting for another 40 to 60 minutes, or until the lamb is done to your taste.

9. A meat thermometer will register 130° to 140° for rare, 140° to 150° for medium, and 150° to 160° for well done.

10. Meanwhile, bring 2 quarts of water and the remaining teaspoon of salt to a boil over high heat.

11. Pour in the the *orzo* in a slow thin stream so that the water does not stop boiling, and cook briskly for about 10 minutes until the *orzo* is tender but still slightly resistant to the bite.

12. Drain in a sieve or colander.

13. When the leg of lamb is done, place it on a large heated platter and let it rest at room temperature for 10 or 15 minutes for easier carving.

14. Meanwhile, pour off all but a thin film of fat from the roasting pan.

15. Stir the tomato purée into the onions, scraping in any brown particles clinging to the bottom and sides of the pan.

16. Stir in the *orzo*, return the pan to the middle shelf of the oven and bake uncovered for 10 to 15 minutes until the *orzo* is heated through.

17. Taste for seasoning.

18. To serve, mound the *orzo* around the leg of lamb and pass the grated cheese separately to be sprinkled over the pasta.

Roast Leg of Lamb with Mint Sauce

To serve 6 to 8

MINT SAUCE
¼ cup water
1 tablespoon sugar
¼ cup finely chopped fresh mint leaves
½ cup malt vinegar

1. Make the mint sauce in advance.
2. Combine the water and sugar in a 1- to 1½ quart saucepan, and bring to a boil over high heat, stirring until the sugar dissolves completely.
3. Remove the pan from the heat, and stir in the mint leaves and vinegar. Taste and add up to 1 more tablespoon of sugar if desired.
4. Set aside at room temperature for 2 or 3 hours.

MEAT
2 tablespoons salt
1 teaspoon finely ground black pepper
1 tablespoon finely cut fresh rosemary or 2 teaspoons dried crushed rosemary
A 5- to 6-pound leg of lamb, trimmed of excess fat, but with the fell (the parchmentlike covering) left on

1. Preheat the oven to 500° (it will take about 15 minutes for most ovens to reach this temperature).
2. Combine the salt, pepper and rosemary in a small bowl, and with your fingers press the mixture firmly into the lamb, coating the entire surface as evenly as possible. For the most predictable results, insert a meat thermometer into the thickest part of the leg, being careful not to touch a bone.
3. Place the leg, fat side up, on a rack in a shallow roasting pan, and roast it uncovered in the middle of the oven for 20 minutes.
4. Reduce the heat to 375° and roast for another 40 to 60 minutes, or until the lamb

is cooked to your taste (basting is unnecessary). A meat thermometer will register 130° to 140° when the lamb is rare, 140° to 150° when medium, and 150° to 160° when well done.
5. Transfer the lamb to a heated platter, and let the roast rest for 15 minutes for easier carving.
6. Stir the mint sauce once or twice, pour it into a sauceboat and serve it separately with the lamb.

Mock Venison

To serve 10 to 12

A 6-pound leg of lamb
½ pound salt pork
1½ cups cider vinegar
1 tablespoon sugar
¾ teaspoon pepper
½ cup seedless raisins
2 garlic cloves, cut in thin slivers
1 tablespoon salt
½ teaspoon ground ginger
¾ cup sliced onions
2 tablespoons vegetable oil
6 cloves
1 cup boiling water
3 tablespoons apricot jam
2 tablespoons flour
1 cup cold water
2 cups canned peach halves
2 tablespoons melted butter
Currant jelly
Parsley sprigs

1. Have the shank cut off the lamb.
2. Cover the salt pork with water, bring to a boil and cook for 5 minutes. Drain, dry and cut it into ½-inch cubes.
3. Mix together the vinegar, sugar and ¼ teaspoon of the pepper.
4. Marinate the pork squares in it for 1 hour.

5. Drain the pork cubes and reserve the marinade.

6. Cut slits in the leg of lamb, and into each insert a pork cube, a raisin and a sliver of garlic.

7. Rub the lamb all over with the salt, ginger and remaining pepper.

8. Spread the onion slices over the lamb, then pour the marinade over it.

9. Marinate in the refrigerator for 48 hours, turning the meat frequently.

10. Preheat the oven to 425°. Drain the lamb well.

11. Heat the oil in a large deep skillet or Dutch oven and brown the lamb.

12. Add the cloves and boiling water, cover and cook over low heat for 2 hours, or until the lamb is tender.

13. Mix together the jam, flour and cold water. Pour the mixture over the lamb.

14. Bake, uncovered, in the oven until the meat is browned and crisp, about 20 minutes.

15. Transfer it to a heated serving dish. Turn the oven down to 400°.

16. Drain the peaches and arrange them on a baking sheet. Brush them with the melted butter.

17. Bake in the oven until they are delicately browned.

18. Fill the peach cavities with currant jelly, arrange them around the lamb, and garnish the platter with parsley sprigs.

Roast Leg of Lamb with Sherry

To serve 6

A 5-pound leg of lamb
3 garlic cloves, slivered
2 teaspoons salt
½ teaspoon black pepper
½ teaspoon rosemary
3 tablespoons butter
2 sliced celery stalks
1 grated carrot
¾ cup chopped onions
¾ cup water
¾ cup dry sherry

1. Preheat the oven to 300°.

2. Make several shallow cuts in the lamb and into them insert the garlic slivers.

3. Season the lamb with the salt, pepper and rosemary.

4. Place it in a roasting pan then dot it with the butter.

5. Surround the lamb with the celery, carrot and onions.

6. Pour the water into the pan.

7. Roast in the oven, allowing 25 minutes per pound. Baste and turn frequently.

8. Add the sherry 30 minutes before the end of the roasting time.

9. Pour off the pan juices and skim the fat.

10. Serve the sauce with the carved lamb.

Spiced Leg of Lamb

Raan   *To serve 6 to 8*

2 tablespoons scraped, finely chopped fresh ginger root
6 medium-sized garlic cloves, peeled and coarsely chopped
The seeds of 2 cardamom pods or ⅛ teaspoon cardamom seeds
A 1-inch piece of stick cinnamon, coarsely crushed with a rolling pin or mallet
8 whole cloves
1 teaspoon cumin seeds
1 teaspoon turmeric
1 teaspoon ground hot red pepper
4 teaspoons salt
¼ cup fresh lemon juice
A 5- to 6-pound leg of lamb, trimmed of all fell (parchmentlike outer covering) and any excess fat
½ cup unsalted, unroasted pistachios
½ cup seedless raisins
¼ cup slivered, blanched almonds
1 cup unflavored yoghurt
¼ cup honey
½ teaspoon saffron threads
3 tablespoons plus 1 cup boiling water

1. Combine the ginger, garlic, cardamom, cinnamon, cloves, cumin, turmeric, hot red pepper, salt and lemon juice in the jar of an elecric blender.
2. Blend at high speed for 30 seconds, then turn off the machine and scrape down the sides of the jar with a rubber spatula.
3. Blend again until the mixture becomes a smooth purée.

4. With a small, sharp knife, make about a dozen slashes 1 inch long and 2 inches deep on each side of the leg of lamb.
5. Rub the spice purée over the entire outer surface of the leg, pressing it as deeply into the slashes as possible.
6. Place the lamb in a heavy casserole large enough to hold it comfortably and set it aside to marinate for 30 minutes at room temperature.
7. Meanwhile purée the pistachios, raisins, almonds and yoghurt in the blender jar, and spread the mixture evenly over the lamb.
8. Drip the honey on top of the leg, cover the casserole tightly, and marinate the lamb in a cool place for about 24 hours, or in the refrigerator for at least 48 hours.
9. Preheat the oven to 350°.
10. Drop the saffron threads into a small bowl, add 3 tablespoons of boiling water, and let them soak for 15 minutes.
11. Pour the saffron and its soaking water over the leg of lamb, and pour the remaining cup of water down the sides of the casserole.
12. Bring to a boil over high heat, cover tightly, and bake the lamb in the middle of the oven for 1½ hours.
13. Then reduce the heat to 250° and bake 30 minutes longer, or until the lamb is tender and shows no resistance when pierced with the point of a small, sharp knife.
14. Remove the casserole from the oven, uncover it, and let the lamb cool in the sauce for 1 hour before serving.

Leg of lamb as it is cooked in India is surprisingly sweet and yet pungent. It is flavored by spices – cardamom, cumin, turmeric and ground hot red pepper.

Broiled Leg of Lamb

To serve 7 or 8

A 6- to 8-pound leg of lamb
1 sliced medium-sized onion
1 sliced carrot
¼ teaspoon dried oregano
½ cup olive oil
1 cup red wine vinegar
Peppercorns
1 garlic clove (optional)
Salt

1. Have the leg of lamb boned, then place it in a large bowl.
2. Sprinkle the onion, carrot and oregano over the lamb.
3. Blend together the oil and vinegar and pour this mixture over the meat.
4. Add a few peppercorns and, if you wish, a clove of garlic.
5. Let the meat stand in the marinade in a cool place for several hours or overnight, turning it occasionally.
6. Preheat the broiling unit and pan.
7. Remove the meat from the marinade but do not dry it.
8. Spread it out flat and put it in the broiler pan about 2½ to 3 inches away from the fire.
9. Broil the lamb for 20 minutes, brush the top side with a little of the marinade, season it with salt and turn the meat over.
10. Brush the top with the marinade and cook for 20 minutes more.
11. Sprinkle the top side with salt and serve the meat on a heated platter.

Marinated Leg of Lamb

Jagnjeći But   *To serve 6 to 8*

A 7-pound leg of lamb, boned and tied
1 teaspoon salt
1 cup vinegar
2 cups water
3 bay leaves
2 cups sliced onions
6 peppercorns
2 sprigs parsley
1½ teaspoon thyme
2 tablespoons lard
4 large fresh tomatoes, coarsely chopped,
 or 1 large can tomatoes, drained
3 slices bacon
Salt

1. Rub the leg of lamb with the salt and put it in an earthenware or enameled casserole.
2. In a saucepan, combine the vinegar, water, bay leaves, onions, peppercorns, parsley and thyme.
3. Over high heat, bring to a boil, cool to lukewarm, then pour over the lamb.
4. Marinate the lamb, uncovered, in the refrigerator for 6 to 24 hours, turning it every couple of hours.
5. Preheat the oven to 350°.
6. Remove the lamb from the marinade and pat it dry with paper towels.
7. Heat the lard in a heavy 12-inch skillet until a light haze forms over it, then add the lamb.
8. Cook it for 15 to 20 minutes, or until it is brown, turning it every 5 minutes with two wooden spoons.

9. Place it in a casserole or roasting pan just large enough to hold it.
10. Strain the marinade into a bowl and add the contents of the strainer, 1½ cups of the marinade and the tomatoes to the casserole.
11. Lay the bacon slices over the lamb.
12. Bring the liquid to a boil on top of the stove, then cook, covered, in the middle of the oven for about 2 hours, checking occasionally to see that the liquid is barely bubbling. (Reduce the heat if necessary.)
13. When the meat shows no resistance when pierced with the point of a small sharp knife, remove it to a platter.
14. Strain the cooking juices through a sieve into a saucepan, pressing down hard on the vegetables before discarding them.
15. Skim the surface fat and bring the juices to a boil on top of the stove. Taste for seasoning.
16. To serve, slice the lamb, and arrange it on a serving platter. Mask the slices with some of the sauce and serve the rest in a sauceboat.

Roasted Leg of Lamb Roll

Cordeiro à Transmontana   *To serve 6 to 8*

¼ **cup finely chopped parsley**
¼ **cup finely cut fresh mint leaves**
2 **tablespoons butter, softened**
2 **tablespoons finely chopped lean bacon**
2 **teaspoons finely chopped garlic**
1 **tablespoon red wine vinegar**

1 **teaspoon paprika**
1 **teaspoon salt**
¼ **teaspoon freshly ground black pepper**
A 6 to 7 **pound leg of lamb, boned, with outer fell and all fat removed**
2 **tablespoons olive oil**

1. In a large bowl, combine the parsley, mint, butter, bacon, garlic, vinegar, paprika, salt and black pepper, and mix them together thoroughly.
2. With a large, sharp knife, open the leg of lamb flat by cutting lengthwise through the thinnest side of the cavity left when the bones were removed.
3. Cut away any clumps of exposed fat from inside the leg and, with the point of the knife, cut ¼ to ½ inch down into the thicker areas so that the lamb lies even flatter.
4. Spread the leg out flat, fat side down, and pat the parsley and mint mixture evenly over the meat.
5. Then, starting at one long side, roll the lamb into a tight cylinder, tucking in the ragged edges of meat. With white kitchen cord, tie the roll securely at two-inch intervals, wrap it loosely in foil or plastic wrap, and refrigerate for at least 12 hours.
6. Preheat the oven to 450°.
7. With a pastry brush, coat the surface of the lamb with the olive oil.
8. Place the meat on a rack in a shallow roasting pan just large enough to hold it comfortably. For the most predictable results, insert a meat thermometer into the center of the meat.
9. Roast uncovered in the middle of the oven for 15 minutes.
10. Then reduce the heat to 350° and continue roasting uncovered 45 minutes to 1 hour, or until the lamb is done to your taste. Basting is unnecessary.
11. Carve the lamb crosswise into ¼-inch-thick slices and arrange them slightly overlapping along the center of a heated platter.
12. Serve at once.

The classic among all lamb dishes is the crown roast, filled with fresh peas, and bones embellished with gay paper frills.

Crown Roast of Lamb

To serve 6 to 8

A crown roast of lamb, consisting of 16 to 18 chops and weighing about 4½ pounds
1 clove garlic, cut into tiny slivers (optional)
2 teaspoons salt
1 teaspoon freshly ground black pepper
1 teaspoon crushed dried rosemary
16 to 18 peeled new potatoes, all about 1½ inches in diameter
3 cups cooked fresh or frozen peas
2 tablespoons melted butter
6 to 8 sprigs of fresh mint

1. Preheat the oven to 475°.
2. With the point of a small, sharp knife make small incisions a few inches apart in the meaty portions of the lamb, and insert in them the slivers of garlic, if you are using it.
3. Combine the salt, pepper and rosemary, and with your fingers pat the mixture all over the bottom and sides of the crown.
4. To help keep its shape, stuff the crown with a crumpled sheet of foil and wrap the ends of the chop bones in strips of foil to prevent them from charring and snapping off.
5. Place the crown of lamb on a small rack set in a shallow roasting pan just large enough to hold it comfortably and roast it in the center of the oven for about 20 minutes.

6. Then turn down the heat to 400° and surround the crown with the new potatoes, basting them with the pan drippings and sprinkling them lightly with salt.
7. Continue to roast the lamb (basting the lamb is unnecessary, but baste the potatoes every 15 minutes or so) for about an hour to an hour and 15 minutes, depending upon how well done you prefer your lamb. Ideally, it should be served when it is still somewhat pink, and should register 140° to 150° on a meat thermometer.
8. When the crown is done, carefully transfer it to a large circular platter, remove the foil and let the lamb rest about 10 minutes to make carving easier.
9. Meanwhile, combine the peas with the melted butter and season them with as much salt as is necessary.
10. Fill the hollow of the crown with as many of the peas as it will hold and serve any remaining peas separately.
11. Put a paper frill on the end of each chop bone and surround the crown with the roasted potatoes.
12. Garnish with mint and serve at once.
13. To carve the lamb, insert a large fork in the side of the crown to steady it and with a large, sharp knife cut down through each rib to detach the chops. Two rib chops per person is a customary portion.

Boiled leg of lamb is at its best simmered in a savory stock with vegetables –
parsnips, carrots, potatoes and celery – and topped with marjoram sauce.

Boiled Lamb in Marjoram Sauce

Gesottenes Lämmernes in Majoran Sauce   To serve 6 to 8

**A 3-pound boned lamb shoulder or leg,
  rolled and tied**
1 large onion, quartered
**3 parsnips, 1 cubed, 2 scraped and cut into
  julienne strips (3 inches long, ½ inch
  wide)**
**5 carrots, 2 cubed, 3 scraped and cut into
  julienne strips (3 inches long, ½ inch
  wide)**
**3 celery stalks, 1 coarsely chopped, cut in-
  to julienne strips (3 inches long, ½ inch
  wide)**
2 quarts water
1½ teaspoons salt
**3 large potatoes (1½ to 2 pounds), peeled
  and sliced lengthwise into ¼-inch strips**
2 tablespoons butter
2 tablespoons flour
¼ teaspoon marjoram
**3 anchovy fillets, drained and finely
  chopped**
1 tablespoon lemon juice
1 tablespoon finely chopped parsley

1. Combine the lamb, onion, the cubed parsnip and carrots, and the chopped celery in a 5-or 6-quart saucepan.
2. Pour in the water and add the salt.
3. Bring to a boil, then lower the heat and simmer, covered, for 2½ hours, or until the lamb shows no resistance when tested with the tip of a sharp knife.
4. When the lamb is almost done, blanch the julienne carrots, parsnips, celery and potatoes by cooking them rapidly for 3 minutes in enough unsalted boiling water to cover them. Drain and set them aside.
5. Transfer the lamb to a heated platter.
6. Pour the stock through a strainer, pressing hard on the vegetables with a wooden spoon before discarding them.
7. Skim off the surface fat and return the stock to the pan. Boil it over high heat, uncovered, until it is reduced to about 3 cups.
8. Meanwhile, in another saucepan, melt the butter, stir in the flour and cook over very low heat until light brown.
9. Add the marjoram, anchovies, lemon juice and half the parsley.
10. Stir in the 3 cups of stock, continuing to whisk over low heat until the sauce is creamy and smooth.
11. Transfer the lamb to the large saucepan or a 4-quart casserole and pour the sauce over it.
12. Bring it a boil, then reduce the heat to low and add the julienne carrots, parsnips, celery and potatoes.
13. Simmer for 10 minutes longer, or until the vegetables are tender but not mushy. Taste for seasoning.
14. Serve the lamb on a platter with the vegetables surrounding it.
15. Pour a few tablespoons of the sauce over the lamb and serve the rest in a sauceboat. Garnish the meat with parsley.

Lamb in Dill Sauce

Dillkött på Lamm   To serve 6 to 8

4 pounds breast or shoulder of lamb, cut in 2-inch cubes
4 to 5 cups water
Bouquet of 1 bay leaf, 5 sprigs dill and 5 sprigs parsley, tied together with a string
1 tablespoon salt
4 whole peppercorns, white if possible

1. In a heavy 4- to 6-quart casserole that is equipped with a cover, cover the lamb with 4 to 5 cups of cold water and bring it to a boil, uncovered, over high heat.
2. Lower the heat to moderate and with a large spoon skim off and discard the scum as it rises to the surface.
3. Add the bouquet and the salt and peppercorns to the pot.
4. Partially cover the pot and simmer the lamb very slowly for about 1½ hours, or until the meat is tender when pierced with the tip of a sharp knife.
5. With a slotted spoon, remove the lamb to a deep heated platter or casserole, cover with foil and keep warm in a 200° oven.

DILL SAUCE
2 tablespoons butter
2 tablespoons flour
2½ cups reduced lamb stock (from above)
3 tablespoons chopped fresh dill
1 tablespoon white vinegar
2 teaspoons sugar
½ teaspoon salt
½ teaspoon lemon juice
Pepper
1 egg yolk, lightly beaten
Dill sprigs
Lemon slices.

1. To make the sauce, strain the lamb stock from the casserole through a fine sieve into a 1½- to 2-quart shallow saucepan and boil it down rapidly over high heat until it is reduced to 2½ cups.

2. Meanwhile, in another 1-quart saucepan, melt the 2 tablespoons of butter.
3. Remove this pan from the heat, stir in the 2 tablespoons of flour, then add all of the reduced lamb stock at once, stirring it rapidly with a wire whisk.
4. Return the pan to the heat and bring the sauce to a boil, whisking constantly, until it is smooth and thick.
5. Simmer the sauce over low heat for about 5 minutes, stirring frequently.
6. Add the chopped dill, vinegar, sugar, salt and lemon juice.
7. Stir a couple of tablespoons of the hot sauce into the beaten egg yolk, then pour this mixture slowly back into the sauce, beating constantly with a wire whisk.
8. Heat through again, but do not let the sauce boil.
9. Taste for seasoning, add salt and pepper if necessary, and strain the sauce through a fine sieve over the lamb.
10. Garnish the platter with additional sprigs of dill and lemon slices, and serve with boiled buttered new potatoes or rice.

Lamb Chops in Wine

To serve 4

3 tablespoons butter
4 thick loin lamb chops
8 small white onions
8 small pieces of carrot
½ cup water
½ pound sliced mushrooms
½ cup white wine
Salt
Pepper
Lemon juice

1. Heat 1 tablespoon of the butter in a large skillet, add the chops and brown them on both sides.

2. Remove the chops, melt the remaining 2 tablespoons of butter in the pan, and brown the onions and carrot pieces over a moderate fire, shaking the pan often to brown them evenly.

3. Stir in the water, scraping the pan to blend in all the particles.

4. Put back the chops, add the sliced mushrooms, white wine, and salt and pepper to taste.

5. Cover and simmer for 30 minutes.

6. Just before serving sprinkle the chops with a little lemon juice.

7. Make a bed of the vegetables and sauce on a hot serving dish. Arrange the chops down the center of the dish and serve immediately.

Lamb Chops in Tomato Sauce

Chuletas de Cordero a la Navarra　　　　*To serve 4*

¼ cup olive oil
8 lean lamb chops, cut ½ inch thick
Salt
Freshly ground black pepper
2 *chorizos,* or substitute ⅓ pound other garlic-seasoned smoked pork sausage

1. Preheat the oven to 375°.

2. In a heavy 10- to 12-inch skillet, heat the oil over high heat until a light haze forms above it.

3. Sprinkle the chops liberally with salt and a few grindings of pepper. Then brown them in the oil, turning them with tongs and regulating the heat so that they color quickly and evenly without burning.

4. Arrange the chops in a baking dish just large enough to hold them comfortably in one layer and set aside.

5. Place the sausages in a 6- to 8 inch skillet and prick them in two or three places with the point of a small, sharp knife.

6. Add enough cold water to cover them completely and bring to a boil over high heat. Then reduce the heat to low and simmer uncovered for 5 minutes.

7. Drain on paper towels, then slice the sausages into ¼-inch-thick rounds. Set aside.

SOFRITO
1 cup finely chopped onions
1 teaspoon finely chopped garlic
½ cup finely diced *serrano* ham, or substitute ⅛ pound prosciutto or other lean smoked ham
4 medium-sized tomatoes peeled, seeded and finely chopped, or substitute 1½ cups finely chopped, drained, canned tomatoes
1 small bay leaf, crumbled
¼ teaspoon thyme, crumbled
½ cup water
1 tablespoon finely chopped parsley

1. To make the *sofrito,* add the onions and garlic to the fat remaining in the skillet and, stirring frequently, cook for 5 minutes, or until the onions are soft and transparent but not brown.

2. Add the ham and cook for a minute or two, then add the tomatoes, bay leaf, thyme and water.

3. Bring to a boil and cook briskly for about 5 minutes, or until most of the liquid in the pan evaporates and the mixture holds its shape lightly in a spoon. Taste for seasoning.

4. Scatter the sausage slices over the chops and spread the *sofrito* evenly over them.

5. Bake uncovered in the middle of the oven for about 20 minutes, or until the chops are tender.

6. Sprinkle them with the parsley and serve at once, directly from the baking dish.

Lamb Chops in Onion Sauce

Hammel Koteletten mit Zwiebelosse To serve 6

**6 shoulder lamb chops, cut ½ inch thick
  and trimmed of excess fat**
Salt
Freshly ground black pepper
4 tablespoons lard
2 tablespoons butter
1½ cups finely chopped onions
1 tablespoon flour
1½ cups heavy cream
⅛ teaspoon ground nutmeg
**¼ pound boiled or baked smoked ham,
  chopped fine (about ½ cup)**

1. Preheat the oven to 350°.
2. Pat the chops completely dry with paper towels and sprinkle them generously on both sides with salt and pepper.
3. In a heavy 12-inch skillet, melt the lard over high heat until a light haze forms above it.
4. Add the chops and brown them well on each side, regulating the heat so that the meat colors quickly and evenly without burning.
5. Transfer the chops to a shallow, flameproof casserole large enough to hold them in one layer.
6. Discard the fat in the skillet, and in its place add the 2 tablespoons of butter. Melt it over moderate heat, and when the foam subsides add the onions.
7. Cook, stirring occasionally, for 8 to 10 minutes, or until the onions are soft, transparent and light brown.
8. Stir in the flour, mix thoroughly, then gradually pour in the cream, stirring constantly with a whisk. Bring to a boil, continuing to stir until the sauce is smooth and thick.
9. Add the nutmeg and taste for seasoning.
10. Then purée the sauce through a coarse sieve set over a bowl, pressing down hard on the onions with the back of a spoon before discarding them, and stir the chopped ham into the sauce.
11. Spoon the sauce over the lamb chops and bring to a simmer over moderate heat.
12. Cover the casserole tightly and bake in the middle of the oven for 15 minutes, or until the chops are tender.
13. Serve the chops directly from the casserole.

Braised Lamb Shanks

To serve 4

3 tablespoons flour
Salt
Paprika
4 lamb shanks, about 1 pound each
2 tablespoons butter
2 tablespoons olive oil
1 large onion, thinly sliced
¾ cup red wine
1¼ cups water
¼ teaspoon chopped fresh rosemary
Pepper

1. Preheat the oven to 375°.
2. Season 1 tablespoon of the flour with salt and a little paprika and lightly dust the shanks.
3. Heat the butter and olive oil in a deep heavy saucepan and brown the shanks all over.
4. Remove them from the pan and lightly brown the onion in the pan juices.
5. Return the meat to the pan, adding the wine, ¾ cup of water and the chopped fresh rosemary. Season with salt and pepper.
6. Cover and cook in the oven for about 2 hours, or until the meat is tender enough to be easily pierced with a fork.
7. Remove the lamb shanks. Blend the remaining flour with the remaining ½ cup of water, add to the pan liquid and stir over the fire until the gravy thickens and comes to a boil.
8. Simmer for 2 to 3 minutes, then strain.
9. The shanks can be served as they are on a hot platter, with the gravy in separate gravy boat; or the meat can be cut from the bones and arranged on a hot serving dish, spooning a little of the gravy over the meat and serving the rest separately.

Lamb Shanks with Tomato Sauce

Lahma Bisalsat Tamatim   *To serve 4*

1 tablespoon olive oil
4 lean, meaty lamb shanks, each about ¾ pound
2 medium-sized onions, cut into ¼-inch-thick slices
1 teaspoon allspice
½ teaspoon ground nutmeg
1 teaspoon salt
Freshly ground black pepper
A pinch of cayenne pepper
9 medium-sized, fresh, ripe tomatoes, peeled, seeded and finely chopped, or substitute 3 cups chopped, drained, canned tomatoes
3 cups water

1. Preheat the oven to 450°.
2. Using a pastry brush apply the tablespoon of olive oil the bottom of a baking dish large enough to hold the lamb shanks comfortably in one layer.
3. Place the shanks in the dish and bake in the middle of the oven for 30 minutes, turning the pieces occasionally so that they color evenly on all sides.
4. Remove the dish from the oven and spread the onion slices over the lamb.
5. Sprinkle them with the allspice, nutmeg, salt, a few grindings of black pepper, cayenne, and spread the tomatoes on top.
6. Pour in the water and bring to a boil on top of the stove.
7. Bake on the lowest shelf of the oven for 1 hour, or until the lamb is tender and shows no resistance when pierced with the point of a small, sharp knife.
8. Serve directly from the baking dish or arrange the shanks on a heated platter and pour the sauce over them.

Roast Lamb Shanks and Lentils

To serve 4

2 cloves garlic cut into paper-thin slivers
4 meaty lamb shanks (about 1 pound each)
Salt
Freshly ground black pepper
3 tablespoons vegetable oil
2 tablespoons butter
½ cup finely chopped onion
2½ cups beef stock, fresh or canned
2½ cups lentils, thoroughly washed and
  drained
1 bay leaf
½ cup chopped scallions
¼ cup chopped fresh parsley

1. Preheat the oven to 350°.
2. With the point of a small, sharp knife, insert 2 or 3 garlic slivers into the meaty portion of each lamb shank. Then sprinkle the shanks generously with salt and a few grindings of black pepper.
3. In a 12-inch heavy skillet, heat the oil over high heat until a light haze forms over it.
4. Add the shanks, and then, over moderate heat, cook them on all sides for about 10 minutes, turning them with tongs. When the shanks are a deep golden brown, transfer them to a rack set in a shallow roasting pan.
5. Roast them in the middle of the oven for about an hour, or until the shanks are tender. Basting is unnecessary.
6. While the shanks are roasting, melt 2 tablespoons of butter over moderate heat in a 2- to 4-quart saucepan.
7. When the foam subsides add the onions and cook them for about 6 minutes, stirring frequently until they are transparent but not brown.
8. Pour in the stock and add the lentils, bay leaf, salt and a few grindings of black pepper.
9. Bring to a boil. Cover the pot and reduce the heat to its lowest point.
10. Simmer the lentils, stirring occasionally, for about 30 minutes, or until they are very tender.
11. To serve, stir into the lentils 2 tablespoons of drippings from the roasting pan and ½ cup of chopped scallions. Taste for seasoning.
12. Arrange the lamb and lentils on a heated platter and sprinkle with parsley.

Roast lamb shanks with lentils make a simple but sustaining winter meal. The lentils are cooked in beef stock with bay leaf and onions.

Lamb curry with a special sauce flavored and thickened with cashews makes a superb winter supper. Originally from India, curries are now international.

Lamb Curry

Korma   *To serve 4*

CURRY
¼ cup untoasted, unsalted cashews
3 dried hot red chilies, stemmed and
  seeded
A 1-inch piece of fresh ginger root, scraped
  and quartered
A 2-inch piece of stick cinnamon, wrapped
  in a kitchen towel and crushed with a
  rolling pin
¼ teaspoon cardamom seeds
3 whole cloves
2 large garlic cloves, peeled
2 tablespoons white poppy seeds
1 tablespoon coriander seeds
1 teaspoon cumin seeds

LAMB
½ teaspoon saffron threads
6 tablespoons *ghee,* or substitute clarified
  butter
1 cup finely chopped onions
2 teaspoons salt

½ cup unflavored yoghurt
1½ pounds lean boneless lamb leg or
  shoulder, cut into 2-inch cubes
2 tablespoons finely chopped fresh coriander
1 tablespoon fresh lemon juice

NOTE: Wear rubber gloves when handling the hot chilies.
1. To make the curry, combine the cashews, chilies, ginger and 1 cup of cold water in the jar of an electric blender.
2. Blend at high speed for 1 minute, or until the mixture is reduced to a smooth purée. Turn the machine off and scrape down the sides of the jar with a rubber spatula.
3. Add the cinnamon, cardamom, cloves, garlic, poppy seeds, coriander seeds and cumin, and blend again until the mixture is completely pulverized. Set the curry aside.
4. Place the saffron in a small bowl, pour in ¼ cup of boiling water, and let it soak for at least 10 minutes.
5. Meanwhile, in a heavy 10- to 12-inch

skillet, heat the *ghee* over moderate heat until a drop of water flicked into it splutters instantly.

6. Add the onions and, stirring constantly, fry for 7 or 8 minutes, until soft and golden brown.

7. Stir in the salt and curry, then add the yoghurt.

8. Stirring occasionally, cook over moderate heat until the *ghee* lightly films the surface.

9. Add the lamb, turning it about with a spoon to coat the pieces evenly.

10. Squeeze the saffron between your fingers, then stir it and its soaking liquid into the skillet.

11. Reduce the heat to low, cover tightly and cook for 20 minutes, turning the lamb cubes over from time to time.

12. Scatter 1 tablespoon of the fresh coriander over the lamb and continue cooking, tightly covered, for 10 minutes more, or until the lamb is tender.

13. To serve, transfer the entire contents of the skillet to a heated platter, and sprinkle the top with lemon juice and the remaining fresh coriander.

Braised Lamb with Anchovy Sauce

Abbacchio alla Cacciatora   *To serve 4*

¼ **cup olive oil**
2 **pounds boneless lamb shoulder, cut in**
   1½-inch chunks
1 **teaspoon finely chopped garlic**
1 **teaspoon dried rosemary, crumbled**
1 **teaspoon salt**
½ **teaspoon freshly ground black pepper**
1 **tablespoon flour**
⅓ **cup red wine vinegar**
1 **cup chicken stock, fresh or canned**
2 **flat anchovy fillets, drained, washed and**
   dried

1. Preheat the oven to 500°.

2. In a heavy 10- to 12-inch skillet, heat the olive oil until a light haze forms over it.

3. Add the lamb, 4 or 5 chunks at a time, and brown it over moderately high heat. As the chunks become richly colored on all sides, transfer them to a heavy 2½- to 3-quart flameproof casserole.

4. Then pour off all but a thin film of fat from the skillet and set the pan aside.

5. Season the lamb with garlic, rosemary, salt and pepper, and sprinkle it with flour, tossing the meat with a wooden spoon to coat the chunks as evenly as possible with the seasonings and flour.

6. Place the casserole in the upper third of the oven and brown the lamb uncovered for 8 to 10 minutes, turning it 2 or 3 times.

7. When no trace of gummy flour remains and the chunks of lamb are lightly crusted, remove the casserole from the oven and reduce the oven heat to 350°.

8. Pour the vinegar into the waiting skillet and boil it briskly over high heat for a minute or two, scraping in any browned bits clinging to the bottom and sides of the pan.

9. Add the chicken stock to the vinegar, bring to a boil, and then pour the liquid over the lamb in the casserole. Cover the casserole and place it in the middle of the oven.

10. Braise the lamb for about 1 hour, or until it is tender when pierced with the tip of a sharp knife. (If the braising sauce seems to be cooking away too fast, add a little more stock, a tablespoon at a time.)

11. Just before serving, ladle 1 or 2 tablespoons of the sauce from the casserole into a small bowl and mix in the chopped anchovies.

12. Stir the anchovy mixture into the casserole and cook for 2 or 3 minutes more.

13. Serve the lamb directly from the casserole or in a deep, heated platter.

Braised Lamb and Eggplant

Khoresh Bademjan   *To serve 4*

1 medium-sized eggplant (about 1 to 1½ pounds)

¼ cup plus 1 teaspoon salt

½ to ¾ cup olive oil

1 medium-sized onion, peeled and cut into ¼-inch-thick slices

1½ pounds lean boneless lamb shoulder, cut into 2-inch cubes

2 cups beef stock, fresh or canned, or 2 cups water

2 tablespoons tomato paste

½ teaspoon turmeric

Freshly ground black pepper

1 medium-sized tomato, cut crosswise into 4 slices

2 tablespoons fresh lemon juice

1 tablespoon bottled pomegranate syrup (optional)

1. With a large, sharp knife peel the eggplant and cut off its stem end.

2. Slice the eggplant lengthwise into quarters, then cut the quarters lengthwise in half to make 8 long strips.

3. Combine 1 quart of water and ¼ cup of the salt in a shallow bowl or baking dish, add the eggplant and turn the strips about with a spoon to moisten them thoroughly with the brine. Soak at room temperature for about 10 minutes.

4. Meanwhile, in a heavy 12-inch skillet, heat ½ cup of olive oil over moderate heat until a light haze forms above it.

5. Add the onions and, stirring frequently, cook for about 10 minutes, or until they are deeply browned.

6. Then transfer them with a slotted spoon to a plate and set aside.

7. Drain the eggplant strips through a sieve and pat them dry with paper towels.

8. Heat the oil remaining in the skillet over high heat.

9. Add the eggplant strips and brown them thoroughly on both sides, adding more oil to the pan if necessary.

10. Transfer the strips to a plate and set them aside.

11. Brown the lamb cubes well in the same pan, again adding more oil if needed.

12. Then add the stock or water, tomato paste, turmeric, the remaining teaspoon of salt, and a few grindings of pepper.

13. Bring to a boil over high heat, meanwhile scraping in the brown particles clinging to the bottom and sides of the pan.

14. Add the reserved onions, reduce the heat to low, and simmer tightly covered for 45 minutes.

15. Arrange the strips of eggplant side by side on top of the lamb and place the tomato slices over them.

16. Pour in the lemon juice and the pomegranate syrup, if you are using it.

17. Cover tightly again and simmer for about 45 minutes longer, or until the eggplant and lamb are tender.

18. Taste for seasoning and serve at once from a deep heated platter or bowl.

Braised Lamb with Kidney Beans

Gormeh Sabzi   *To serve 6*

7 cups water
1½ teaspoons salt
1 cup dried, red kidney beans
¼ cup olive oil
2 pounds lean boneless lamb, preferably
   lamb shoulder, trimmed of excess fat and
   cut into 2-inch cubes
1 pound lamb bones, sawed, not chopped,
   into 2 or 3 pieces
¼ cup finely chopped onions
2 cups finely chopped parsley
¼ cup finely chopped leeks, including 1
   inch of the green tops
¼ cup finely cut fresh dill or 2 tablespoons
   dried dill weed
3 tablespoons finely cut fresh mint or 1
   tablespoon dried mint
4 teaspoons ground fenugreek seeds
1 tablespoon turmeric
1 teaspoon oregano
Freshly ground black pepper
1 cup fresh lemon juice

1. Bring 4 cups of the water and 1 teaspoon of the salt to a boil in a heavy 2- to 3-quart saucepan.
2. Drop in the kidney beans and boil them for 2 minutes.
3. Remove the pan from the heat and let the beans soak for 1 hour.
4. Then return to low heat and simmer uncovered for 1 hour, or until the beans are somewhat tender but still intact.
5. Drain the beans thoroughly in a large sieve or colander and set them aside.
6. Meanwhile, in a heavy 10- to 12-inch skillet, heat the oil over high heat until a light haze forms above it.
7. Brown the lamb and bones in the hot oil in 2 or 3 batches, turning the pieces frequently with a spoon and regulating the heat so that they color deeply and evenly without burning. As they brown, transfer the lamb cubes and bones to a heavy 4- to 5-quart casserole.
7. Drop the onions into the fat remaining in the skillet and, stirring frequently, cook over moderate heat for about 5 minutes, or until they are soft and transparent but not brown.
8. Add the parsley, leeks, dill, mint, fenugreek, turmeric, oregano, the remaining ½ teaspoon of salt and a few grindings of pepper.
9. Stirring constantly, cook the mixture briskly until almost all of the liquid in the pan has evaporated.
10. Transfer the entire contents of the skillet to the casserole with the lamb.
11. Add the remaining 3 cups of water and stir until the ingredients are well mixed.
12. Bring to a boil over high heat, reduce the heat to low, and simmer tightly covered for 1 hour, or until the lamb is tender and shows no resistance when pierced with the point of a small, sharp knife.
13. Add the beans to the lamb mixture, cover and simmer for 15 minutes.
14. Then stir in the lemon juice and simmer tightly covered for 15 minutes more.
15. Taste for seasonings. Serve at once.

Braised Lamb with Lemon Sauce

Abbacchio Brodettatto   *To serve 6*

2 ounces fresh pork fat, diced (about ½ cup)
2 pounds boneless lamb shoulder, cut in 1½-inch chunks
½ teaspoon salt
Freshly ground black pepper
3 tablespoons flour
½ teaspoon finely chopped garlic
½ cup dry white wine
3 cups beef stock, fresh or canned
1 bay leaf
2 egg yolks
1 tablespoon lemon juice
2 tablespoons finely chopped fresh parsley

1. Preheat the oven to 500°.
2. Fry the diced fat in a heavy 10- to 12-inch skillet over high heat, stirring frequently, until the dice are crisp and brown.
3. Remove them with a slotted spoon and discard them.
4. In the fat remaining in the skillet, brown the lamb, 4 or 5 chunks at a time. As the chunks become golden brown on all sides, transfer them to a heavy 2½-to 3-quart flameproof casserole.
5. Then pour off all but a thin film of fat from the skillet and set the pan aside; it will be used again.
6. Sprinkle the lamb with salt and a few grindings of pepper, and add the flour, tossing the meat with a wooden spoon to coat the chunks as evenly as possible with the seasoning and flour.
7. Place the casserole in the upper third of the oven and brown the lamb uncovered, turning it 2 or 3 times, for about 10 minutes, or until no trace of gummy flour remains and the chunks are lightly crusted.
8. Remove from the oven, and reduce the heat to 350°.
9. In the fat remaining in the skillet, cook the garlic over moderate heat, stirring constantly for 1 minute.
10. Pour in the wine and boil briskly until it is reduced to ¼ cup. Scrape in any browned bits clinging to the bottom and sides of the skillet.
11. Stir in the stock and bring to a boil, then pour the entire contents of the skillet over the chunks of lamb in the casserole.
12. Bring the casserole to a boil on top of the stove.
13. Add the bay leaf, cover the casserole and cook in the middle of the oven for 1½ hours, or until the lamb is tender.
14. Transfer the lamb to a heated platter, and cover it lightly with foil to keep it warm.
15. Strain the braising stock through a fine sieve into a small saucepan. Let the stock settle, then skim the fat from the surface.
16. In a small bowl, beat the egg yolks and lemon juice together with a whisk, and stir in 2 tablespoons of the hot stock.
17. Add 2 more tablespoons of stock, stirring constantly, then whisk the now warmed egg-yolk-and-lemon mixture into the stock remaining in the pan.
18. Over moderate heat, bring this sauce to a boil, stirring constantly, and cook it for 30 seconds, or until it is thick enough to coat the wires of the whisk lightly. Taste for seasoning.
19. Pour the sauce over the lamb, sprinkle with parsley and serve.

Lamb and Celery

Khoresh Karafs   *To serve 4 to 6*

½ cup olive oil
2 medium-sized onions, peeled and cut in ⅛-inch-thick slices
1½ pounds lean boneless lamb shoulder, trimmed of excess fat and cut into 2-inch cubes
1 pound lamb bones, sawed, not chopped, into 2-inch pieces
2 cups water

1 teaspoon turmeric
1 teaspoon salt
6 large celery stalks
¼ cup fresh lemon juice

1. In a heavy 10- to 12-inch skillet, heat ¼ cup of the olive oil over moderate heat until a light haze forms above it.
2. Add the onions and, stirring frequently, cook for about 10 minutes, or until they are deeply browned.
3. With a slotted spoon, transfer the onions to a heavy 3- to 4-quart casserole and set them aside.
4. Brown the lamb and bones in the oil remaining in the skillet, turning the pieces frequently with a spoon and regulating the heat so they color deeply and evenly without burning.
5. When all the lamb and bones are brown, add them to the casserole and pour the water into the skillet.
6. Bring it to a boil over high heat, meanwhile scraping in any brown particles clinging to the bottom and sides of the pan.
7. Then pour it over the lamb in the casserole and stir in the turmeric and salt. Set the skillet aside.
8. Bring the casserole to a boil, reduce the heat to low and simmer tightly covered for 1 hour.
9. Meanwhile, wash the celery under cold running water.
10. With a small, sharp knife, trim off the root ends and scrape the heavy strings from the back of each stalk. Cut away the leaves and chop them finely. Cut the stalks crosswise into 3-inch pieces and then lengthwise into strips about ¼ inch wide.
11. In the reserved skillet, heat the remaining ¼ cup of oil over moderate heat.
12. Add the strips of celery and, stirring frequently, cook for about 10 minutes, or until they are a delicate brown, then stir them into the casserole.
13. Add the celery leaves and lemon juice

and simmer tightly covered for about 30 minutes longer, or until the lamb is tender. Taste for seasoning.

Lamb with String Beans

Lubya Khadra Billahma To serve 4

2 pounds green string beans, trimmed and cut into 2-inch lengths
3 tablespoons olive oil
1 pound boneless stewing lamb, cut into 1-inch cubes
1 cup finely chopped onions
6 medium-sized, fresh, ripe tomatoes, peeled, seeded and coarsely chopped, or substitute 2 cups chopped, drained, canned tomatoes
1 teaspoon salt
Freshly ground black pepper
½ teaspoon ground nutmeg, preferably freshly grated
½ teaspoon ground allspice

1. Spread the beans evenly in the bottom of a heavy 4- to 6-quart casserole, and set aside.
2. In a heavy 10- to 12-inch skillet, heat the oil over moderate heat until a light haze forms above it.
3. Add the lamb and brown it, turning the pieces frequently with a spoon and regulating the heat so they color deeply and evenly without burning. As they brown, transfer the pieces of lamb to the casserole, placing them on top of the beans.
4. Pour off all but a thin film of fat from the skillet, and in it cook the onions over moderate heat for 5 minutes, or until they are soft and transparent but not brown.
5. Spread the onions over the lamb and cover them with the tomatoes.
6. Sprinkle the top with salt, a few grindings of the pepper, the nutmeg and allspice.
7. Place the casserole over low heat, cover tightly, and simmer without stirring for 1 hour, or until the beans and meat are tender.
8. Serve at once.

Broiled skewered lamb, the traditional shish kebab, is varied by adding swordfish and tomatoes with peppers. A delicious rice accompanies.

Broiled Skewered Lamb

Şiş Kebabi   *To serve 4*

1 large onion, peeled and cut into ⅛-inch-thick slices and separated into rings
2 tablespoons olive oil
4 tablespoons fresh lemon juice
2 tablespoons salt
½ teaspoon freshly ground black pepper
2 pounds lean boneless lamb, preferably from the leg, trimmed of excess fat and cut into 2-inch cubes
1 large, firm, ripe tomato, cut crosswise into four slices
1 large green pepper, cut into quarters, seeded and deribbed
2 tablespoons heavy cream

1. Drop the onion rings into a deep bowl and sprinkle them with the olive oil, lemon juice, salt and pepper.
2. Add the lamb and turn the pieces about with a spoon to coat them well.
3. Marinate at room temperature for at least 2 hours, or in the refrigerator for 4 hours, turning the lamb occasionally.
4. Light a layer of coals in a charcoal broiler and let them burn until a white ash appears on the surface, or preheat a stove broiler to its highest point.
5. Remove the lamb from the marinade and string the cubes tightly on 3 or 4 long skewers, pressing them firmly together.
6. Thread the tomato slices and green pep-

per quarters alternately on a separate skewer.

7. If you are broiling the lamb in a stove, suspend the skewers side by side across the length of a roasting pan deep enough to allow a 1-inch space below the meat.

8. Brush the meat evenly on all sides with the cream.

9. Broil 4 inches from the heat, turning the skewers occasionally, until the vegetables brown richly and the lamb is done to your taste. For pink lamb, allow about 10 minutes; for well-done lamb, allow about 15 minutes.

10. Watch the vegetables carefully; they will take less time to cook than the lamb.

11. Slide the lamb off the skewers onto heated individual plates.

12. Serve with the broiled tomato and green pepper.

Baked Lamb and Wheat

To serve 8 to 10

WHEAT MIXTURE
1 pound *burghul* (fine crushed wheat)
2 pounds lean twice-ground lamb
½ cup grated onions
2 teaspoons salt
½ teaspoon black pepper
¼ teaspoon cinnamon
¼ cup ice water

NOTE: *Burghul* is available in Middle East or other specialty food shops.

1. Soak the wheat in cold water to cover for 30 minutes, kneading it several times.

2. Drain thoroughly, then mix in the lamb, onions, salt, pepper and cinnamon.

3. Knead for a few minutes, then put through the fine blade of a food chopper, adding ¼ cup ice water as you grind.

FILLING
1 tablespoon butter
¾ cup chopped onions
½ pound ground lamb
½ teaspoon salt
¼ teaspoon black pepper
¼ cup pine nuts
½ cup melted butter

1. Preheat the oven to 400°.

2. Melt the butter in a skillet; brown the onions in it.

3. Add the lamb, salt and pepper. Cook, stirring frequently, for 5 minutes.

4. Add the pine nuts. Cook, stirring frequently, until mixture is browned.

5. Pat half the wheat mixture into a greased 9-by-12-inch baking pan.

6. Spread the filling over it. Cover with the remaining wheat mixture, pressing down until firm.

7. With a sharp knife, cut diagonal lines across the top to form a diamond pattern.

8. Pour the melted butter over the top.

9. Bake at 400° for 30 minutes.

10. Reduce heat to 350° and bake 30 minutes longer.

11. Cut into squares and serve. This dish may be eaten hot or cold.

A Middle Eastern specialty, *kibbi*, or lamb paste, is stuffed with ground lamb and pine nuts. The patties are cooked in olive oil just before eating.

Lamb Patties

Kibbi Bissaniyyeh   To serve 6

KIBBI NAYYA
1½ cups fine *burghul* (crushed wheat)
1 pound lean boneless lamb, preferably leg
  of lamb, finely ground 3 times
¼ teaspoon ground allspice
A pinch of ground nutmeg, preferably
  freshly grated nutmeg
A pinch of cayenne pepper
2 teaspoons salt
Freshly ground black pepper

1. Place the *burghul* in a bowl or pan, pour in enough cold water to cover it completely and let it soak for about 10 minutes. Then drain it in a sieve or colander lined with a double thickness of dampened cheesecloth.
2. Wrap the *burghul* in the cheesecloth and squeeze it dry.
3. Drop the *burghul* into a deep mixing bowl, add the lamb and, moistening your hands from time to time with cold water, knead until the mixture is smooth.
4. Knead in the allspice, nutmeg, cayenne, salt and a few grindings of pepper and taste for seasoning.

STUFFING
2 tablespoons olive oil
2 tablespoons pine nuts (pignolia)

2 tablespoons finely chopped onions
¼ pound lean boneless lamb, preferably
** leg of lamb, coarsely ground**
⅛ teaspoon ground allspice
½ teaspoon salt
Freshly ground black pepper
1 cup oil

1. In a heavy 7- to 8-inch skillet, heat the 2 tablespoons of olive oil over moderate heat until a light haze forms above it.
2. Drop in the pine nuts and brown them lightly. With a slotted spoon, transfer the nuts to a plate.
3. Add the onions to the oil remaining in the skillet and, stirring constantly, cook for 5 minutes, or until they are soft and transparent but not brown.
4. Add the lamb and, mashing it frequently with the back of a spoon to break up any lumps, cook until all traces of pink disappear.
5. Tip the pan and drain off any excess fat.
6. Stir the pine nuts, allspice, salt and a few grindings of pepper into the lamb mixture, taste for seasoning and set aside off the heat.
7. Moistening your hands with cold water from time to time, divide the *Kibbi nayya* into 6 equal portions and roll them into egg-shaped patties about 4 inches long and 2½ inches in diameter in the middle.
8. With your forefinger, make a tunnel-like pocket about 3 inches deep and 1 inch across lengthwise into each patty, starting from one of the tapered ends.
9. Gently press about 2 tablespoons of the stuffing mixture into each pocket and, dipping your hands in cold water, reshape the patty around the stuffing to enclose it completely.
10. In a heavy 10- to 12-inch skillet, heat the cup of olive oil over high heat until a light haze forms above it.
11. Add the stuffed lamb patties and fry them for about 15 minutes, turning them occasionally with a spoon and regulating the heat so that they color evenly on all sides without

burning.
12. The patties are done when the lamb shows no trace of pink when pierced gently with the point of a sharp knife. Serve at once.

Turkish Meatballs

Kadin Budu   To make about 16 meatballs

1 pound lean ground lamb
½ cup finely chopped onions
¼ cup uncooked long- or medium-grain
** rice**
1 tablespoon salt
½ teaspoon freshly ground black pepper
1 cup olive oil or vegetable oil
2 eggs, lightly beaten

1. Combine the meat, onions, rice, salt and pepper in a deep bowl.
2. With a large spoon or your hands, mix the ingredients together and knead vigorously until they are well blended.
3. A tablespoon at a time roll the mixture into balls about 1 inch in diameter and shape them into egglike ovals.
4. In a heavy 12-inch skillet, bring 2 cups of water to a boil over high heat.
5. Add the meatballs and return the water to a boil. Reduce the heat to low and simmer uncovered for 30 minutes, adding boiling water if necessary to keep the balls covered.
6. With a slotted spoon, transfer the meatballs to a plate.
7. Pour the water from the skillet, add the oil in its place, and heat over moderate heat until a light haze forms above it.
8. With tongs, dip the balls in the eggs and drop them into the hot oil. Fry the meatballs over high heat for 5 to 8 minutes until they brown on all sides.
9. Drain on paper towels and serve.

Shepherd's Pie

To serve 6

Flank of lamb
1 onion, sliced
3 potatoes, peeled and diced
2 carrots, scraped and diced
1 tablespoon of flour
Salt
Pepper

1. Cover the lamb with cold water and cook until tender.
2. Remove the bones and the fat and cut the meat into small pieces.
3. Let the broth cool and remove the fat. Add the onion to the broth and bring to a boil.
4. Add the potatoes and carrots and cook until the vegetables are nearly done, about 12 minutes.
5. Add the lamb.
6. When the potatoes are cooked thoroughly, thicken the broth with a thin paste of the flour mixed with a little water.
7. Season with salt and pepper.

PASTRY
1 cup flour
⅛ teaspoon salt
⅓ cup shortening
2 tablespoons ice water

1. Sift together the flour and salt. Add half the shortening and chop fine, using two knives.
2. Add the remaining shortening and chop, leaving quite large lumps which make flakes when rolled out.
3. Add about two tablespoons of ice water to hold the mixture together.
4. Turn out on lightly floured board and roll thin.
5. Preheat the oven to 450°.
6. Turn the lamb stew into a 9-inch casserole, cover with the pastry and bake about 12 minutes or until well browned.

Pork

Crown Roast of Pork

To serve 10 to 12

STUFFING
3 tablespoons butter
¾ cup finely chopped onion
¼ cup finely chopped celery
½ cup peeled, cored and coarsely diced
tart apples
½ cup fresh bread crumbs
1 pound ground pork (the crown roast trim-
ming plus extra pork, if necessary)
½ pound well-seasoned sausage meat
½ cup finely chopped parsley
½ teaspoon sage
1½ teaspoons salt
Freshly ground black pepper

A crown roast of pork, consisting of 22
chops and weighing 8 to 9 pounds.

1. Preheat the oven to 350°.
2. For the stuffing, melt the butter over moderate heat in an 8- to 10-inch skillet.
3. When the foam subsides, add the onion and cook, stirring frequently, for about 5 minutes, then add the celery and apples.
4. Cook without browning about 5 minutes longer. Scrape the contents of the pan into a large mixing bowl.
5. Add the bread crumbs, ground pork, sausage meat, parsley, sage, salt and a few grindings of black pepper. With a large spoon, mix all the ingredients together.
6. Fill the center of the crown with the stuffing, mounding it slightly. Cover it with a round of foil and wrap the ends of the chop bones in strips of foil to prevent them from charring and snapping off.
7. Place the crown on a rack in a shallow roasting pan just about large enough to hold it comfortably, and roast it in the center of the oven, undisturbed, for about 3 hours, or until a meat thermometer, if you have used one, reads 170° to 175°.
8. One half hour before the pork is done, remove the circle of foil from the top of the stuffing to allow the top to brown.
9. Carefully transfer the crown to a large, heated, circular platter, strip the foil from the ends of the chops and replace it with paper frills.
10. Let the crown rest for about 10 minutes before carving and serving.

Glazed Roast Loin of Pork

Rôti de Porc Boulangère   *To serve 6*

2 teaspoons salt
1 teaspoon coarsely ground black pepper
2 teaspoons finely cut fresh rosemary or
    1½ teaspoons dried rosemary, crumbled
A 3-pound center-cut pork loin with the
    chine bone (backbone) sawed through but
    still attached, and circumference of loin
    tied in 2 or 3 places
3 onions, coarsely chopped
2 carrots, cut in 1-inch chunks
Bouquet garni made of 4 parsley sprigs and
    1 bay leaf, tied together
2 tablespoons butter
2 medium onions, thinly sliced
6 large firm boiling-type potatoes, cut in
    ¼-inch slices
Salt
Freshly ground black pepper
½ cup heated chicken stock, fresh or
    canned
1½ cups hot beef or chicken stock, fresh
    or canned, or a combination of both
2 tablespoons finely chopped fresh parsley

1. Preheat the oven to 475°.
2. Combine the salt, pepper and rosemary, and press the mixture firmly into the pork roast.
3. Place the seasoned pork, fat side up, in a heavy casserole just large enough to hold the pork.
4. Roast uncovered on the middle shelf of the oven, turning the meat over 2 or 3 times, for 20 to 30 minutes, or until the pork is lightly browned.
5. Then reduce the oven to 325°.
6. Scatter the chopped onions, carrots and the *bouquet garni* around the pork, cover the casserole, and roast for 40 minutes longer, basting the pork every 10 minutes with the pan juices.
7. Meanwhile butter the bottom and sides of a shallow baking-and-serving dish about 12

inches long and 1½ to 2 inches deep.
8. Melt 2 tablespoons of butter in an 8- to 10-inch skillet, and in it cook the onions over moderate heat, stirring frequently, for 10 minutes, or until they are limp and lightly colored.
9. When the pork is ready, spread the potato slices over the bottom of the baking dish and season with salt and pepper.
10. Scatter the onions over the potato slices and pour in the heated stock.
11. Place the pork loin on top and moisten both the pork and the potatoes with 2 or 3 tablespoons of fat skimmed from the drippings in the casserole.
12. Roast uncovered in the bottom third of the oven for another 1¼ hours, or until the pork is crusty and glazed, and the vegetables are tender and brown.
13. While the pork is roasting, add 1½ cups of stock to the drippings left in the casserole.
14. Bring to a boil over high heat and cook for 5 minutes, stirring frequently and scraping in any browned bits that cling to the bottom and sides of the pan.
15. Strain the mixture through a fine sieve into a saucepan, pressing down hard on the vegetables before discarding them.
16. Skim off the surface fat. Season with salt and pepper. Set aside in the pan.
17. To serve, transfer the roast to a carving board, cut off the strings and slice the roast into 8 chops.
18. Reheat the sauce made from the casserole drippings.
19. Return the chops to the baking dish and arrange them in a line over the potatoes and onions.
20. Moisten the pork with a little sauce and dust the potatoes with parsley.
21. Serve the remaining sauce in a sauceboat.

Pork Roast with Paprika and Capers

Geschmorter Schweinsbraten mit Kapern   *To serve 6*

4 tablespoons lard
A 3-pound boneless loin of pork (about 5 pounds with bone in)
¾ cup finely chopped onions
¾ cup diced carrots (1½-inch chunks)
1 teaspoon sweet Hungarian paprika
1 cup chicken or beef stock
Salt
Freshly ground black pepper
2 tablespoons flour
1 cup sour cream
1 tablespoon finely chopped parsley
1 teaspoon capers, drained, dried and chopped
1 tablespoon caraway seeds

1. In a 4-quart casserole, heat the lard until a light haze forms over it.
2. Add the pork and, over high heat, turning it with a fork, brown it on all sides – about 10 or 15 minutes altogether – then remove it and set it aside.
3. Preheat the oven to 350°.
4. Pour off all but a thin film of the fat and add the onions. Cook them about 8 minutes over medium heat, or until they are lightly colored.
5. Add the carrots and cook 2 or 3 minutes longer.
6. Off the heat, stir in the paprika. Continue to stir until the vegetables are coated.
7. Pour in the stock and bring it to a boil, stirring in any brown bits that cling to the bottom and sides of the pan.
8. Return the pork to the pan, fat side up, salt and pepper it, and bring the liquid to a boil again.
9. Cover tightly and braise the pork in the middle of the oven for 1½ hours, or until thoroughly cooked and tender. Baste it occasionally with the pan juices.
10. Transfer the pork to a heated platter.
11. Pour the contents of the pan into a sieve set over a saucepan, pressing down hard on the vegetables before discarding them. Skim off as much of the surface fat from the pan liquid as possible and bring the sauce to a simmer on top of the stove.
12. With a wire whisk, beat the flour and sour cream together in a bowl, then beat the mixture into the pan.
13. Bring the sauce to a simmer once more and add the parsley, capers and caraway seeds. Taste for seasoning.

Pork Loin Stuffed with Prunes and Apples

Mørbrad med Svedsker og Aebler   *To serve 6 to 8*

4½- to 5-pound boned loin of pork, center cut
12 medium-sized pitted prunes
1 large apple, peeled, cored and cut into 1-inch cubes
1 teaspoon lemon juice
Salt
Freshly ground black pepper
3 tablespoons butter
3 tablespoons vegetable oil
¾ cup dry white wine
¾ cup heavy cream
1 tablespoon red currant jelly

1. Place the prunes in a saucepan, cover with cold water, and bring to a boil.
2. Remove from the heat and let the prunes soak in the water for 30 minutes. Then drain, pat dry with paper towels, and set aside.
3. Sprinkle the cubed apple with lemon juice to prevent discoloring.
4. With a strong, sharp knife, make a pocket in the pork by cutting a deep slit down the length of the loin, going to within ½ inch of the two ends and to within 1 inch of the other side.
5. Season the pocket lightly with salt and pepper and stuff it with the prunes and apples, sewing up the opening with strong kitchen thread.
6. Tie the loin at 1-inch intervals to keep its shape while cooking. An alternative method of stuffing the loin is described opposite.
7. Preheat the oven to 350°.
8. In a casserole equipped with a cover and just large enough to hold the loin of pork comfortably, melt the butter and oil over moderate heat.
9. When the foam subsides, add the loin, turning it from time to time with 2 wooden spoons. It should take about 20 minutes to brown the loin evenly on all sides.
10. With a bulb baster or large spoon, remove all the fat from the pan.
11. Pour in the wine, stir in the heavy cream, whisking briskly, and bring to a simmer on top of the stove.
12. Cover the pan and cook in the center of the oven for 1½ hours, or until the meat shows no resistance when pierced with the tip of a sharp knife.
13. Remove the loin from the pan and let it rest on a heated platter while you finish the sauce.
14. Skim the fat from the liquid in the pan and bring the liquid to a boil.
15. When it has reduced to about 1 cup, stir in the red currant jelly, reduce the heat and, stirring constantly, simmer briefly until the sauce is smooth. Taste for seasoning and pour into a heated sauceboat.
16. Cut away the strings from the loin, then carve the meat into 1-inch slices.
17. Each slice of meat will surround a portion of the stuffing.
18. Pass the sauce separately.

Pierce a loin of pork with a long, sharp tool – here, a steel knife sharpener

Fill the tunnel you have made in the loin with prunes and apples

Pack in the fruit tightly with a blunt, round tool, such as a wooden spoon handle. Each slice of the roasted loin *(right)* has its own built-in decorative core of prunes and apples.

Sweet-and-sour-pork – a photograph of which is superimposed here on an old Chinese painting – is made with pork, green pepper, carrot, sugar and vinegar.

Sweet-and-Sour Pork

T'ien-suan-ku-lao-jou To serve 2 to 4

1 pound lean boneless pork, preferably
  butt
1 egg, lightly beaten
1 teaspoon salt
¼ cup cornstarch
¼ cup flour
¼ cup chicken stock, fresh or canned
3 cups peanut oil, or flavorless vegetable
  oil
SAUCE
1 tablespoon peanut oil, or flavorless
  vegetable oil
1 teaspoon finely chopped garlic
1 large green pepper, seeded, deribbed and
  cut in ½ inch squares
1 medium carrot, scraped and sliced into
  2-inch strips ¼ inch wide and ¼ inch
  thick
½ cup chicken stock, fresh or canned
4 tablespoons sugar
4 tablespoons red-wine vinegar
1 teaspoon soy sauce
1 tablespoon cornstarch dissolved in 2
  tablespoons cold water

PREPARE AHEAD. 1. Trim the pork of any excess fat and, with a cleaver or sharp knife, cut the meat into 1-inch cubes.
2. In a large bowl, mix together the egg, ¼ cup cornstarch, ¼ cup flour, ¼ cup chicken stock and salt. Set aside.
3. For the sauce, have the oil, garlic, green pepper, carrot, chicken stock, sugar, vinegar, soy sauce and cornstarch mixture within easy reach.

TO COOK: 1. Just before cooking, add the pork cubes to the egg and flour mixture, and stir until each piece of meat is well coated. Preheat the oven to 250°.
2. Pour the 3 cups of oil into a wok and set it over high heat.
3. When the oil almost begins to smoke or reaches 375° on a deep-frying thermometer, drop in half of the coated pork cubes one by one.
4. Fry for 5 to 6 minutes, regulating the heat so that the pork turns a crisp, golden brown in that period without burning.
5. Remove the pork with a strainer or slotted spoon to a small baking dish and keep it warm in the oven.
6. Fry the other half and add to the first batch.
7. To make the sauce, pour off any oil remaining in the wok or use a 10-inch skillet. Set the pan over high heat for about 30 seconds.
8. Pour in the tablespoon of oil, swirl it about in the pan and heat for another 30 seconds, turning the heat down to moderate if the oil begins to smoke.
9. Add the garlic, then the green pepper and carrot, and stir-fry for 2 to 3 minutes until the pepper and carrot darken somewhat in color. Be careful not to let them burn.
10. Pour in the ½ cup of chicken stock, the sugar, vinegar and soy sauce, and bring to a boil.
11. Boil rapidly for about 1 minute, or until the sugar has thoroughly dissolved. Immediately give the cornstarch mixture a quick stir to recombine it and add it to the pan.
12. Cook a moment longer, stirring constantly.
13. When the sauce is thick and clear, pour the entire contents of the pan over the fried pork and serve at once.

VARIATION: Sweet-and-sour shrimp is made in precisely the same way – with identical batter and sauce. Shell and devein 1 pound of fresh or defrosted frozen shrimp and substitute them for the pork in this recipe.

Pork Chops with Mustard Sauce

Côtes de Porc Braisées à la Moutarde To serve 6

6 center cut loin pork chops, cut 1½ inches thick
Salt
Freshly ground black pepper
Flour
2 tablespoons butter
3 tablespoons vegetable oil
1½ cups thinly sliced onions
3 tablespoons wine vinegar (preferably white)
***Bouquet garni* made of 2 parsley sprigs and 1 bay leaf, tied together**
¾ cup heavy cream
2 teaspoons Dijon-style prepared mustard
A few drops of lemon juice
Fresh parsley sprigs

1. Preheat the oven to 325°.
2. Season the chops generously with salt and pepper, dip them in flour, then vigorously shake off all but a light dusting.
3. In a heavy 10- to 12-inch skillet, melt the butter with the oil over moderate heat.
4. When the foam subsides, brown the chops for about 3 minutes on each side, or until they are a rich golden color.
5. As the chops brown, remove them from the skillet with tongs and place them in a shallow flameproof casserole large enough to hold them all, preferably in one layer.
6. After the chops are browned, pour off all but a thin film of fat from the skillet.
7. Add the onions and cook them over moderate heat, stirring frequently, for 5 minutes, or until they are soft and lightly browned.
8. Stir in the wine vinegar, bring it to a boil and scrape up any browned bits that cling to the bottom and sides of the skillet.
9. Cook the vinegar almost completely away, then spoon the onions and juices over the chops, and add the *bouquet garni*.

10. Bring the casserole to a sizzle on top of the stove, cover it tightly and bake it on the middle shelf of the oven for 10 minutes.
11. With a bulb baster or large spoon, baste the chops with the juices that have accumulated in the casserole or, if there is not enough of these, with 2 or 3 tablespoons of heated chicken stock.
12. Bake for 10 minutes longer, then turn the chops over and baste them again.
13. After another 10 minutes test the chops by piercing one near the bone with the tip of a sharp knife; if the juices that run out are yellow with no traces of pink, the chops are done.
14. With tongs, transfer the chops to a heated platter and cover or set in a 200° oven to keep warm.
15. Tip the casserole and skim as much fat as possible from the surface of the drippings.
16. Pour in the cream and bring the sauce to a boil over high heat, stirring constantly.
17. When the sauce has thickened sufficiently to coat the back of a spoon lightly, remove the casserole from the heat and stir in the mustard and lemon juice.
18. Strain the sauce through a fine sieve directly over the chops, pressing down hard on the onions with the back of a spoon before discarding them.
19. Garnish the chops with parsley and serve at once.

1 small bay leaf
3 medium-sized tomatoes peeled, seeded and finely chopped, or substitute 1 cup chopped, drained, canned tomatoes
½ cup finely chopped *serrano* ham, or substitute ⅛ pound prosciutto or other lean smoked ham
½ cup dry white wine
1 cup water
1 hard-cooked egg, finely chopped
2 tablespoons finely chopped parsley
12 pitted Spanish black olives, cut lengthwise into halves

Pork Chops with Tomatoes and Black Olives

Lomo de Cerdo a la Zaragozana　　　　　*To serve 6*

6 lean loin pork chops, cut about 1 inch thick (about 3 pounds)
Salt
Freshly ground black pepper
½ cup flour
¼ cup olive oil
1 cup finely chopped onions
½ teaspoon finely chopped garlic

1. Sprinkle the pork chops liberally with salt and a few grindings of pepper. Dip them in flour and shake each one vigorously to remove the excess.
2. In a heavy 10- to 12-inch skillet, heat the oil over high heat until a light haze forms above it.
3. Add the chops (in 2 batches if necessary) and brown them well, turning them with tongs and regulating the heat so that they color quickly and evenly without burning.
4. Transfer the chops to a plate and add the onions, garlic and bay leaf to the fat remaining in the skillet.
5. Cook over moderate heat for 5 minutes, or until the onions are soft and transparent but not brown.
6. Add the tomatoes and ham, raise the heat and cook briskly, stirring frquently until most of the liquid in the pan evaporates and the mixture is thick enough to hold its shape lightly in a spoon.
7. Stir in the wine, water, egg, parsley and olives, and bring to a boil again.
8. Return the chops to the skillet, and baste them thoroughly with the sauce.
9. Cover tightly, reduce the heat to its lowest point, and simmer for about 30 to 40 minutes, or until the chops are tender.
10. To serve, arrange the chops attractively on a heated platter and pour the sauce over them.

Pork Chops Braised in White Wine

Costolette di Maiale alla Modenese　　　*To serve 4*

1 teaspoon dried sage leaves, crumbled
1 teaspoon dried rosemary leaves,
**　crumbled**
1 teaspoon finely chopped garlic
1 teaspoon salt
Freshly ground black pepper
4 center-cut loin pork chops, about 1 inch
**　thick**
2 tablespoons butter
1 tablespoon olive oil
¾ cup dry white wine
1 tablespoon finely chopped fresh parsley,
**　preferably the flat-leaf Italian type**

1. Combine the sage, rosemary, garlic, salt and a few grindings of pepper and press a little of this mixture firmly into both sides of each pork chop.
2. In a heavy 10- to 12-inch skillet, melt the butter with the olive oil over moderate heat.
3. When the foam subsides, place the chops in the hot fat and brown them for 2 or 3 minutes on each side, turning them carefully with tongs. When the chops are golden brown, remove them from the pan to a platter.
4. Pour off all but a thin film of fat from the pan, add ½ cup of the wine and bring to a boil.
5. Return the chops to the pan, cover and reduce the heat to the barest simmer.
6. Basting with the pan juices occasionally, cook the chops for 25 to 30 minutes, or until they are tender when pierced with the tip of a sharp knife.
7. Transfer the chops to a heated serving platter, skim off all the fat from the braising liquid and pour the remaining ¼ cup of wine into the skillet.
8. Boil it briskly over high heat, stirring and scraping in any browned bits that cling to the bottom and sides of the pan, until it has reduced to a few tablespoons of syrupy glaze. Remove the skillet from the heat.
9. Taste for seasoning and stir in the parsley.
10. Pour the sauce over the pork chops and serve.

Pork Chops with Tomato and Garlic Sauce

Costolette di Maiale alla Pizzaiola　　　*To serve 6*

4 tablespoons olive oil
6 center-cut loin pork chops, cut 1 to 1½
**　inches thick**
1 teaspoon finely chopped garlic
½ teaspoon dried oregano, crumbled
¼ teaspoon dried thyme, crumbled
½ bay leaf
½ teaspoon salt
½ cup dry red wine
1 cup drained canned tomatoes, puréed

through a sieve or food mill
1 tablespoon tomato paste
½ pound green peppers, seeded and cut in 2-by-¼-inch strips (about 1½ cups)
½ pound fresh mushrooms, whole if small, quartered or sliced if large

1. In a heavy 10- to 12-inch skillet, heat 2 tablespoons of olive oil until a light haze forms over it.
2. Brown the chops in this oil for 2 or 3 minutes on each side and transfer them to a plate. Pour off almost all of the fat.
3. In it cook the garlic, oregano, thyme, bay leaf and salt for 30 seconds, stirring constantly.
4. Add the wine and boil briskly to reduce it to about ¼ cup, scraping in any bits of meat or herbs in the pan.
5. Stir in the tomatoes and tomato paste and return the chops to the skillet. Baste with the sauce, cover, and simmer over low heat, basting once or twice, for 40 minutes.
6. Meanwhile, heat the remaining oil in another large skillet.
7. Fry the green peppers in the oil for about 5 minutes, stirring frequently.
8. Add the mushrooms and toss them with the peppers for a minute or two, then transfer them to the pan with the pork chops.
9. Cover and simmer for 5 minutes. Simmer uncovered, stirring occasionally, for 10 minutes longer, until the pork and vegetables are tender and the sauce is thick.
10. To serve, arrange the chops on a heated platter and spoon the vegetables and sauce over them.

Pork with Cumin, Coriander and Lemon

Rojões Comino   *To serve 4*

2 pounds lean boneless pork, cut into 1-inch cubes
1 tablespoon lard
¾ cup dry white wine
1½ teaspoons ground cumin seed
½ teaspoon finely chopped garlic
1 teaspoon salt
Freshly ground black pepper
5 thin lemon slices, quartered
2 tablespoons finely chopped fresh coriander (*cilantro*)

1. Pat the pork cubes thoroughly dry with paper towels.
2. In a heavy 10- to 12-inch skillet, melt the lard over high heat until it splutters.
3. Add the pork cubes and brown them, turning the cubes frequently with a large spoon and regulating the heat so that they color quickly and evenly without burning.
4. Stir in ½ cup of wine, the cumin, garlic, salt and a liberal grinding of pepper.
5. Bring to a boil, then cover the skillet, reduce the heat to low and simmer for 25 minutes, or until the pork is tender and shows no resistance when pierced with the tip of a small, sharp knife.
6. Add the remaining ¼ cup of wine and the lemon slices and cook over high heat, turning the meat and lemon pieces constantly, until the sauce thickens ever so slightly.
7. Stir in the coriander and taste for seasoning.

Pork chops in aspic, a German specialty, are enhanced by floral patterns of carrots, cucumbers, hard-cooked egg white and tomatoes.

Pork Chops in Aspic

Sülzkotelett   *To serve 6*

A 2-pound loin of pork, center cut, with the backbone (chine) sawed through but left attached and tied to the loin in 2 or 3 places
2 cups dry white wine
½ cup white wine vinegar
5½ cups cold water
1 medium-sized onion, peeled and pierced with 2 whole cloves
1 scraped carrot, cut into ¼-inch slices
2 celery stalks, including the leaves, coarsely chopped
10 parsley sprigs
1 bay leaf
1 teaspoon salt
¼ teaspoon freshly ground black pepper
2 envelopes unflavored gelatin
2 egg whites, beaten to a froth
Garnish as desired with thinly sliced and fancifully cut flowers made from any combination of cooked or raw carrots, drained and rinsed sweet gherkins, drained and rinsed pimientos, drained and rinsed pickled cauliflower, blanched scallion or leek tops, peeled cucumber, peeled and seeded tomato, and whites of hard-cooked eggs

1. In a deep, heavy casserole or a soup pot just large enough to hold the meat comfortably, combine the pork loin, wine, vinegar and 5 cups of cold water.
2. Bring to a boil over high heat, meanwhile skimming off the foam and scum that rise to the surface.
3. Reduce the heat to low and add the onion, carrot, celery, parsley, bay leaf, salt and pepper.
4. Cover the casserole and simmer the pork for 1½ hours, or until it is tender and shows no resistance when pierced with the tip of a sharp knife.
5. Transfer the pork to a plate and let it cook to room temperature. Then cover it with aluminum foil or plastic wrap and refrigerate. (If you plan to use the carrot slices to garnish the chops in the finished dish, reserve them on the plate with the pork loin.)
6. Strain the cooking stock through a fine sieve into a large bowl, discarding the vegetables and herbs.
7. With a large spoon skim the surface of all fat. There should be about 5 cups of stock. If more, boil briskly, uncovered, until reduced to the required amount.
8. Prepare the aspic in the following fashion: Sprinkle the gelatin into the ½ cup of cold water and let it soften for 5 minutes.
9. Then, in a 3- to 4-quart saucepan, combine it with the stock and add the beaten egg whites.
10. Over high heat, bring the stock to a boil, meanwhile stirring constantly with a whisk. When the stock begins to froth and rise, remove the pan from the heat.
11. Let it rest for 5 minutes, then pour it into a large sieve lined with a damp kitchen towel and set over a large bowl.
12. Allow the aspic to drain through without disturbing it at any point, then taste for seasoning (it will probably need more salt) and set it aside. Do not refrigerate.
13. Carefully carve the pork loin into 6 chops about ½ inch thick.
14. Cut the meat and fat away from the bones and trim the chops into neat, symmetrical cutlets.
15. Pour a layer about ⅛ inch thick of the aspic into each of 6 cutlet molds or into a shallow baking dish large enough to hold the cutlets comfortably in one layer.

(continued on page 54)

16. Chill in the refrigerator until firmly set.

17. Decorate the surface of the set aspic with the garnish of your choice and carefully place the chops on top of it.

18. Pour enough liquid aspic into the mold or baking dish to come halfway up the sides of the chops and refrigerate again until the aspic is firm. (This step is necessary to prevent the chops from rising to the surface of the molds when the remaining aspic is added.)

19. When the chops are firmly anchored, cover them completely with liquid aspic and refrigerate for at least 4 hours, until firm.

20. Any remaining aspic may be chilled in a flat pan or dish at the same time and used chopped or cut into decorative shapes as a garnish when the chops are served.

21. To unmold chops from individual molds, run a small sharp knife around the side of each mold, then dip the bottom into hot water for a few seconds. Wipe the mold dry and turn it out on a chilled serving plate.

22. The chops in the baking dish may be served directly from the dish or you may unmold them in the following fashion: Run a sharp knife around the sides of the dish and dip the bottom in hot water for a few seconds. Place a flat, shallow platter upside down over the dish and, grasping the platter and dish firmly together, invert them. Rap them on a table and the aspic should slide out easily.

Fancy-looking molded aspics like the pork cutlets opposite are surprisingly simple to make. The trick is to use layers of liquid aspic and let each become firm before you add another. First, pour a film of aspic into the mold and refrigerate until firm *(top)*. Add the decorations *(center)*. Place a cutlet on top and pour in enough aspic to cover it halfway. Refrigerate until set, then fill the mold with aspic and refrigerate again *(bottom)*. When all the layers are chilled, the mold is ready to turn out and serve.

Pork Chops with Paprika and Dill

To serve 4 to 6

8 pork chops, ¾ inch thick (trimmed)
Salt
Freshly ground black pepper
Flour
3 tablespoons lard
1½ cups finely chopped onions
¼ teaspoon finely chopped garlic
3 tablespoons sweet Hungarian paprika
1 cup chicken stock, fresh or canned, or water
⅓ cup heavy sweet cream
⅓ cup sour cream
2 tablespoons flour
3 tablespoons finely chopped fresh dill

1. Sprinkle the chops generously with salt and a few grindings of pepper, then dip them in the flour and shake off the excess.
2. In a 12-inch skillet, heat the lard over high heat until a light haze forms over it.
3. Add the pork chops to the skillet and cook them 3 to 4 minutes on each side. Transfer the chops to a platter.
4. Add the onions and garlic to the fat remaining in the pan, and cook them for 8 to 10 minutes, or until the onions are lightly colored.
5. Off the heat, stir in the paprika, continuing to stir until the onions are well coated.
6. Return the skillet to the heat, pour in the stock or water and bring it to a boil, stirring in any brown bits that cling to the pan.
7. Return the chops to the skillet, reduce the heat to its lowest point, cover tightly and simmer the chops for 1 hour, or until they are tender, then arrange them on a heated platter.
8. Combine the sweet cream and the sour cream in a mixing bowl, then with a wire whisk, beat in the flour. While still beating, pour this mixture into the skillet.
9. Stirring constantly, simmer for 2 to 3 minutes, or until the sauce is thick and smooth.
10. Add the chopped dill and taste for seasoning.

Barbecued Spareribs

To serve 4 to 6

¼ cup vegetable oil
1 teaspoon garlic, minced
2 medium onions, finely chopped
1 six-ounce can tomato paste
¼ cup white vinegar
1 teaspoon salt
1 teaspoon basil or thyme
¼ cup strained honey
½ cup beef stock
½ cup Worcestershire sauce
1 teaspoon dry mustard
4 pounds spareribs

1. Heat the vegetable oil over high heat in a 10- or 12-inch skillet.
2. When a light haze forms above it, add the garlic and onions, and cook, stirring frequently, for 3 to 4 minutes without letting the onions brown.
3. Combine the tomato paste and the vinegar, and then add it to the skillet. Stir in the salt, basil or thyme, the honey, beef stock, Worcestershire sauce and mustard.
4. Mix thoroughly and simmer uncovered over low heat for 10 to 15 minutes. Remove from heat.
5. Preheat the oven to 400°.
6. Place the spareribs fat side up on a rack set in a shallow roasting pan and with a pastry brush thoroughly coat the surface of the meat with the barbecue sauce.
7. Bake in the middle of the oven for 45 minutes to 1 hour, basting thoroughly with the barbecue sauce every 10 minutes or so.
8. When the spareribs are brown and crisp, cut into individual portions and serve at once.

Barbecued spareribs are crisp and succulent when they are seasoned the Chinese way, with honey and soy sauce, and cooked suspended from a rack in the oven.

Chinese Barbecued Spareribs

K'ao-pai-ku   *To serve 4 to 6*

2 pounds spareribs in one piece

MARINADE
¼ **cup soy sauce**
2 tablespoons honey
2 tablespoons *hoisin* sauce
2 tablespoons white vinegar
1 tablespoon Chinese rice wine, or pale dry sherry
1 teaspoon finely chopped garlic

1 teaspoon sugar
2 tablespoons chicken stock, fresh or canned
Canned plum sauce

PREPARE AHEAD: 1. With a cleaver or large, sharp knife, trim any excess fat from the spareribs. If the breastbone is still attached, use a cleaver to chop it away from the ribs and discard it. Place the spareribs in a long, shallow dish, large enough to hold them comfortably.

2. In a small bowl, combine the soy sauce, honey, *hoisin* sauce, vinegar, wine, garlic,

sugar and chicken stock. Stir until they are well mixed. Pour the sauce over the spareribs, baste them thoroughly and let them marinate for 3 hours at room temperature (6 hours if refrigerated), turning them over in the marinade and basting them every hour or so.

TO COOK: 1. Preheat the oven to 375°.
2. To catch the drippings of the spareribs as they roast, and to prevent the oven from smoking as well, fill a large shallow roasting pan or baking dish with water and place it on the lowest rack of the oven. Insert the curved tips of two or three S-shaped hooks – such as curtain hooks or 5-inch lengths of heavy-duty wire or even unpainted coat hangers bent into shape – at each end of the spareribs.
3. As if hanging a hammock, use the curved ends of the hooks to suspend the ribs from the uppermost rack of the oven directly above the pan of water. Roast the ribs undisturbed for 45 minutes.
4. Then raise the oven heat to 450° and roast about 15 minutes longer, or until the spareribs are crisp and a deep, golden brown.
5. To serve, place the ribs on a chopping board and, with a cleaver, separate the strip into individual ribs. If the ribs are large, chop them each in half crosswise.
6. Serve hot or cold with plum sauce.

Spareribs with Pickle Sauce

Schweinerippchen mit Gewürgurkensosse   *To serve 4*

2 pounds spareribs, cut into serving pieces
1 teaspoon salt
Freshly ground black pepper
2 tablespoons lard
1 cup finely chopped onions
2 whole allspice and 1 clove, crushed together with a mortar and pestle or wrapped in a towel and crushed with a rolling pin
1 small bay leaf
1 tablespoon flour
2 tablespoons tomato purée
1 cup finely diced dill pickle
2 cups water

1. Sprinkle the spareribs on both sides with the salt and a few grindings of black pepper.
2. In a heavy 12-inch skillet melt the lard over high heat until a light haze forms above it.
3. Add the spareribs and brown them thoroughly on both sides regulating the heat so that they color evenly without burning. Remove them to a plate.
4. To the fat remaining in the skillet, add the onions, the crushed allspice and clove and the bay leaf, then stir in the flour and tomato purée. Mix vigorously with a wooden spoon until the ingredients are thoroughly combined.
5. Add the pickle and then pour in the 2 cups of water.
6. Bring to a boil, meanwhile stirring with a whisk until the sauce thickens slightly.
7. Reduce the heat to low and return the browned spareribs to the skillet.
8. Baste them well with the sauce and cover the pan. Basting occasionally, simmer for an hour until the ribs are tender and can easily be pierced with the tip of a small, sharp knife. Remove the bay leaf.
9. To serve, arrange the spareribs on a large, heated platter and pour the sauce over them.

Spareribs with Fermented Black Beans

Tou-sh'ih-pai-ku To serve 2

1 pound lean spareribs
1 large clove garlic, crushed and peeled
1 tablespoon peanut oil, or flavorless
  vegetable oil
1 tablespoon soy sauce
1 teaspoon sugar
1 tablespoon fermented black beans,
  chopped
½ cup cold water
1 teaspoon cornstarch dissolved in 1
  tablespoon cold chicken stock, fresh or
  canned, or cold water

PREPARE AHEAD: 1. With a cleaver or large, sharp knife, separate the spareribs and chop them crosswise into 1½-inch lengths.
2. Have the spareribs, and the oil, soy sauce, sugar, fermented black beans and ½ cup of water within easy reach.

TO COOK: 1. Set a 12-inch wok or 10-inch skillet over high heat for 30 seconds.
2. Pour in the oil, swirl it about in the pan and heat for another 30 seconds, turning the heat down if the oil begins to smoke.
3. Add the spareribs and stir-fry them for 3 to 4 minutes until they are lightly browned on both sides.
4. Add the garlic, soy sauce, sugar, black beans and water, and stir to coat the spareribs.
5. Bring to a boil, cover the pan and reduce the heat to low. Simmer for about an hour turning the spareribs occasionally.
6. To serve, arrange the spareribs on a heated platter.
7. Skim and discard the surface fat from the sauce and remove the garlic. Give the cornstarch mixture a quick stir to recombine it and pour it into the pan.
8. Cook, stirring, for a few seconds until the sauce thickens and clears. Then pour it over the ribs and serve at once.

Pork Loin with Sweet Red Peppers

Lombo de Porco com Pimentos Vermelhos To serve 4 to 6

1 tablespoon finely chopped garlic
1 teaspoon salt, preferably coarse
  salt
½ teaspoon freshly ground black pepper
2 pounds boneless pork loin, cut into
  ¼-inch-thick slices
¼ cup lard
4 medium-sized sweet red peppers, seeded,
  deribbed and cut lengthwise into ½-inch-
  wide strips, or substitute 1½ cups drained,
  canned pimientos, cut lengthwise into
  ½-inch strips
1 cup dry white wine
½ cup chicken stock, fresh or canned
1 lemon, cut lengthwise into 8 wedges

The sweetness of peppers melds with pungent garlic-marinated pork and lemon
in the Portuguese dish called *lombo de porco com pimentos vermelhos doces.*

1. With a mortar and pestle or the back of a large heavy spoon, mash the garlic, salt and pepper together to a smooth paste.

2. Lightly spread the pork slices with the paste, place them in a bowl and toss with a spoon.

3. Cover tightly and marinate at room temperature for 2 or 3 hours, or in the refrigerator for 6 hours, turning the pork about in the bowl from time to time.

4. In a heavy 10- to 12-inch skillet, melt the lard over high heat.

5. Brown the pork in the hot fat (in two or three batches if necessary), turning the slices with tongs and regulating the heat so that the slices color quickly and evenly on both sides without burning. As they brown, transfer them to a plate.

6. Add the red peppers (not the pimientos) to the fat remaining in the pan and, stirring frequently, cook them for about 5 minutes, or until they are well coated with the fat but not brown.

7. Transfer the peppers to the plate with the meat.

8. Pour off all but a thin film of fat from the skillet and add the wine and stock. Bring to a boil over high heat, meanwhile scraping into the liquid any brown particles clinging to the bottom and sides of the pan.

9. Return the pork and peppers to the skillet, cover tightly, and reduce the heat to low.

10. Simmer for about 20 minutes, stir in the canned pimientos if you are using them, and cook for 5 more minutes, or until the pork is tender and shows no resistance when pierced with the point of a small, sharp knife.

11. With a slotted spoon, transfer the pork and peppers to a deep, heated platter.

12. Bring the liquid remaining in the skillet to a boil over high heat, stirring constantly and cook briskly until it thickens lightly. Taste for seasoning, then pour the sauce over the meat.

13. Serve garnished with lemon wedges.

Sausage and Oyster Loaf

To serve 6

1 pound pork sausage meat
1 pint raw oysters, ground
2 cups soft bread crumbs
2 eggs, lightly beaten
Hollandaise sauce

1. Preheat the oven to 350°.
2. Combine the sausage meat, ground oysters, bread crumbs and eggs in a large mixing bowl, and blend the ingredients together thoroughly.
3. Place the mixture in a loaf pan and bake for 45 minutes, or until the meat leaves the edge of the pan but is still moist.
4. Drain occasionally with a bulb baster to remove excess fat.
5. Remove the loaf from the pan, slice it, and serve with hot hollandaise sauce.

Bratwurst in Sweet-Sour Sauce

Süss-saure Bratwurst   *To serve 4*

8 bratwurst, separated
1 tablespoon dried black currants
4 whole allspice, pulverized with a mortar and pestle
2 cups cold water
1 tablespoon butter
2 tablespoons flour
2 teaspoons sugar
½ teaspoon salt
1 tablespoon fresh lemon juice

1. Place the bratwurst, currants and allspice in a 2- to 3-quart saucepan and pour in the water.
2. Bring to a boil over high heat, reduce the heat to low and cover the pan.
3. Simmer for 20 minutes, then set the sausages aside on a plate and cover with foil to keep them warm.

4. Let the cooking liquid settle for a minute or two, and skim as much of the fat from the surface as possible.
5. In a heavy 8- to 10-inch skillet, melt the butter over moderate heat. Stir in the flour and cook, stirring constantly, for 3 to 4 minutes, or until the mixture colors slightly. Be careful it doesn't burn.
6. Pour in 1 cup of the reserved cooking liquid including the currants. Stirring constantly with a whisk, bring the sauce to a boil.
7. When it is thick and smooth, reduce the heat to low, stir in the sugar and salt and simmer for 3 to 4 minutes.
8. Slice the sausages into ¼-inch rounds, add them to the sauce and simmer only long enough to heat them through.
9. Just before serving, stir in the lemon juice and taste for seasoning.
10. Transfer the entire contents of the skillet to a large, deep serving platter and serve at once.

Bratwurst in Sour-Cream Sauce

Bratwurst mit saurer Sahnensosse   *To serve 4*

8 bratwurst sausages, separated
2 tablespoons butter
¼ cup cold water
1 tablespoon flour
½ teaspoon salt
1 cup sour cream

1. Drop the bratwurst into 2 quarts of boiling water, remove from the heat, and let the sausages soak for 5 minutes.
2. Drain and pat the bratwurst dry with paper towels.
3. Melt the butter over moderate heat in a heavy 10- to 12-inch skillet, add the bratwurst and cook, turning them frequently with tongs

German sausages come in a wide variety of flavors. All of these contain pork.
The one at the upper right is bratwurst, for which a recipe appears on this page.

until they are a golden brown on all sides.
4. Add the ¼ cup of water to the skillet, reduce the heat, and simmer, uncovered, for 15 to 20 minutes, turning the bratwurst over after 10 minutes. Replenish the water with a few tablespoons of boiling water if the cooking water boils away.
5. Transfer the sausages to a plate, and cover them with foil.
6. With a whisk, beat the flour and salt into the sour cream.
7. Then, a few tablespoons at a time, stir the

sour-cream mixture into the liquid remaining in the skillet.
8. Cook over low heat, stirring constantly, for 5 to 8 minutes, until the sauce is smooth and slightly thickened. Do not let it boil.
9. Slice the sausages into ¼-inch rounds, drop them into the skillet, baste with the sauce and simmer only long enough to heat the bratwurst through.
10. Transfer the entire contents of the skillet to a large, deep platter and serve immediately.

Smoked Bacon with Onions and Apples

Äppel-Fläsk   *To serve 4*

2 to 4 tablespoons butter
1 pound Canadian bacon
2 large onions, thinly sliced
2 large red, tart cooking apples, unpeeled,
  cored and cut in ½-inch-thick rings
Freshly ground black pepper

1. Melt 2 tablespoons of butter in a heavy 10- to 12-inch skillet, and when the foam subsides, add the bacon. Fry 5 to 10 minutes, or until the bacon is lightly browned.
2. Remove from the skillet with a slotted spatula and set aside on paper towels to drain.
3. Fry the onion slices for 6 to 8 minutes in the fat remaining in the skillet, adding more butter if necessary.
4. When the onions are soft and transparent, add the apple rings and cover the pan.
5. Simmer over low heat for 5 to 10 minutes, shaking the pan gently at intervals to prevent the apples from sticking.
6. When the apple rings are sufficiently cooked (they should offer little or no resistance when pierced with the tip of a sharp knife), return the drained bacon to the skillet.
7. Cover the pan and simmer an additional 3 to 5 minutes, or until the bacon is heated through.
8. Grind black pepper liberally over the top and serve the *äppel-fläsk* directly from the pan as a luncheon entrée or Sunday night supper.

Easy to prepare, *äppel-fläsk*, a Swedish dish, combines onions and apples with Canadian bacon, sautéed in a heavy skillet and sprinkled with pepper.

lard over moderate heat.

3. Add the onions and carrots and cook over moderate heat, stirring frequently for 8 to 10 minutes, or until the vegetables are soft and light brown.

4. With a rubber spatula, scrape the entire contents of the skillet into a heavy casserole or roasting pan just large enough to hold the pork comfortably.

5. Place the pork loin, fat side up, on top of the vegetables and strew the crushed juniper berries around the pork.

6. Pour in the 4 cups of water and roast uncovered in the middle of the oven, basting occasionally with the cooking juices, for 1½ hours, or until the pork is golden brown. (If you prefer to use a meat thermometer, insert it into the pork loin before placing the loin in the casserole. Be sure the tip of the thermometer does not touch any bone. Roast the pork until the thermometer reaches a temperature of 175°.)

7. Cut away the strings and carve the pork into ½-inch-thick chops.

8. Arrange the slices attractively in slightly overlapping layers on a large heated platter. Cover and set aside.

9. Strain the pan juices through a fine sieve set over a bowl, pressing down hard on the vegetables with the back of the spoon before discarding them.

10. Skim as much fat as possible from the surface, then measure the juices. If there is more than 1½ cups, boil briskly over high heat until the juices are reduced to that amount; if there is less, add water.

11. Bring the pan juices to a boil over moderate heat in a small saucepan.

12. Give the cornstarch mixture a quick stir to recombine it and add it to the pan. Cook, stirring constantly, until the sauce clears and thickens slightly.

13. Moisten the meat slices with a few spoonfuls of the sauce and serve the rest in a heated sauceboat.

Roast Smoked Pork Loin

Kasseler Rippenspeer *To serve 4 to 6*

2 tablespoons lard
1 cup coarsely chopped onions
1 cup coarsely chopped carrots
A 3½ to 4 pound smoked pork loin in one piece, with the backbone (chine) sawed through at ½-inch intervals, but left attached and tied to the loin in 2 or 3 places
4 whole juniper berries, coarsely crushed with a mortar and pestle or wrapped in a towel and crushed with a rolling pin
4 cups cold water
2 teaspoons cornstarch dissolved in 1 tablespoon cold water

1. Preheat the oven to 350°.

2. In a heavy 8- to 10-inch skillet, melt the

Roast Fresh Ham with Crackling

Flaeskesteg med Svaer   *To serve 8 to 10*

½ fresh ham (butt or shank) weighing about 6 pounds or 6 pounds shoulder of pork with the rind on
Coarse salt or substitute regular salt
Freshly ground black pepper

1. Preheat the oven to 300°.
2. Using a sharp, heavy knife, cut deeply through the rind and fat until you reach the meat, making the incisions ½ inch apart lengthwise and crosswise. Rub salt and pepper liberally into these gashes.
3. Insert a meat thermometer into the thickest part of the ham and place it on a rack set in a shallow roasting pan just large enough to hold the meat comfortably.
4. Roast slowly 4 to 4½ hours, or until the meat thermometer reads 180°. Do not baste the meat. When roasted, the meat should be moist and tender, and the rind (or crackling) very crisp.
5. Let the roast rest outside the oven for 10 to 15 minutes for easier carving.
6. A little of the crackling should be included in each serving of meat.

1. Preheat the oven to 350°.
2. Place the slices of ham in a baking dish and put them aside.
3. Heat the cream in the top of a double boiler.
4. Add the diced cheese, lemon juice, Worcestershire sauce, mustard and a few grains of cayenne and paprika.
5. Cook, stirring constantly, until the cheese is melted.
6. Cover the ham slices with the cheese sauce and bake in the oven until the cheese is lightly browned.

Ham Baked with Cheese

To serve 4

4 slices cooked ham, cut ½ inch thick
½ cup light cream
½ pound American cheese, diced
2 tablespoons lemon juice
½ teaspoon Worcestershire sauce
½ teaspoon French mustard
Cayenne pepper
Paprika

Braised Fresh Ham

Falscher Wildschweinbraten   *To serve 6 to 8*

2 cups dry red wine
½ cup red wine vinegar
1 cup finely grated onions
15 whole juniper berries, crushed with a mortar and pestle or wrapped in a towel and crushed with a rolling pin
2 tablespoons grated fresh lemon peel
6 small bay leaves, coarsely crushed
2 teaspoons dried tarragon
1 teaspoon ground cloves
1 teaspoon ground allspice
1 teaspoon ground ginger
1 teaspoon freshly ground black pepper
A 5- to 6-pound fresh ham, rind removed and the ham trimmed of fat
1 tablespoon salt
2 tablespoons lard
2 cups water
3 tablespoons flour
3 tablespoons cold water

1. For the marinade pour the wine and vinegar into a mixing bowl and stir in the grated onions, juniper berries, grated lemon peel, bay leaves, tarragon, cloves, allspice, ginger and black pepper.
2. Place the ham in a deep dish just large enough to hold it comfortably and pour the marinade over it.
3. Cover with foil and marinate in the refrigerator for two days, turning it over once or twice a day.
4. Preheat the oven to 325°.
5. Remove the ham from the marinade, and dry it thoroughly with paper towels, brushing off any bits of onion or herbs clinging to it. Rub the salt evenly into its surface.
6. Strain the marinade into a bowl or saucepan, pressing down hard with a spoon on the solid ingredients to extract all their liquid before throwing them away.
7. In a heavy casserole or Dutch oven just large enough to hold the ham comfortably, melt the lard over high heat until a light haze forms above it.
8. Add the ham and brown it well on all sides, turning the ham frequently and regulating the heat so the meat colors quickly and evenly without burning. Transfer the ham to a plate.
9. Combine the strained marinade with 2 cups of water and pour the mixture into the casserole.
10. Bring the liquid to a boil over high heat, meanwhile scraping in any brown bits clinging to the bottom and sides of the casserole.
11. Return the ham to the casserole, cover tightly, and bake in the middle of the oven for about 2 hours, basting it every 30 minutes or so with the cooking liquid. The ham is done when it can easily be pierced with the tip of a sharp knife. (You may use a meat thermometer, if you like, for more predictable results. After the ham is browned, insert the thermometer into the thickest part without letting the tip touch any bone. Roast until the thermometer reads 170° to 175°.)
12. Transfer the ham to a heated platter and set it aside to rest for 10 to 15 minutes for easier carving.
13. Meanwhile, strain the cooking liquid into a small saucepan and skim off as much fat as possible from the surface. Measure the liquid, then boil it briskly to reduce it to 2 cups.
14. Reduce the heat to low.
15. Make a smooth paste of the flour and 3 tablespoons of cold water and, with a whisk or spoon, stir it gradually into the simmering liquid.
16. Cook, stirring frequently, for about 10 minutes, or until the sauce thickens slightly. Taste for seasoning.
17. To serve, carve the ham into ¼-inch slices and arrange the slices attractively in overlapping layers on a large heated platter.
18. Serve the sauce separately in a sauceboat.

Baked
Bourbon-glazed Ham

To serve 12 to 14

**A 12- to 14-pound smoked ham, processed,
  precooked variety**
¾ cup bourbon whiskey
2 cups dark brown sugar
1 tablespoon dry mustard
¾ cup whole cloves
2 navel oranges, peeled and sectioned

1. Preheat the oven to 325°.
2. Place the ham fat side up on a rack set in a shallow roasting pan large enough to hold the ham comfortably.
3. Bake in the middle of the oven, without basting, for two hours, or until the meat can be easily pierced with a fork. For greater cooking certainty, insert a meat thermometer in the fleshiest part of the ham before baking it. It should register between 130° and 140° when the ham is done.
4. When the ham is cool enough to handle

A uniquely American delight, this 14-pound ham is garnished with oranges and glazed with cloves, brown sugar, mustard – and bourbon whiskey.

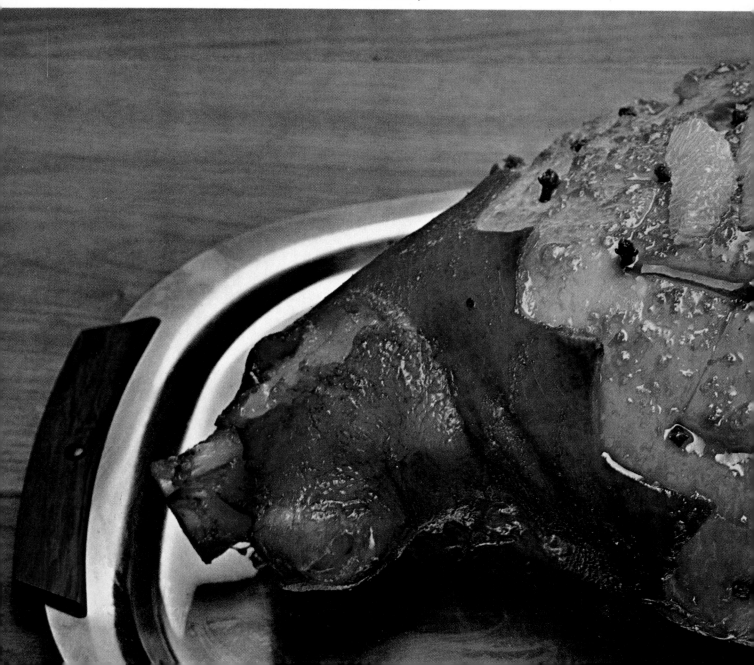

comfortably, cut away the rind with a large, sharp knife. Then score the ham by cutting deeply through the fat until you reach the meat, making the incisions ½ inch apart lengthwise and crosswise.

5. Return the ham to the rack in the pan and raise the oven heat to 450°.

6. With a pastry brush, paint the ham on all sides with ½ cup of the whiskey. Then combine the sugar and mustard and ¼ cup of whiskey, and pat the mixture firmly into the scored fat.

7. Stud the fat at the intersections or in the center of each diamond with a whole clove, and arrange the orange sections as decoratively as you can on the top of the ham with toothpicks or small skewers to secure them.

8. Baste lightly with the drippings on the bottom of the pan and bake the ham undisturbed in the hot oven for 15 to 20 minutes, or until the sugar has melted and formed a brilliant glaze.

Fresh Ham
Braised in Marsala

Prosciutto Fresco Brasato al Marsala   *To serve 6*

1 cup dry Marsala
¼ cup olive oil
2 teaspoons lemon juice
2 bay leaves, crumbled
A 4- to 6-pound half of fresh ham
½ cup coarsely chopped onions
¼ cup coarsely chopped carrots
¼ cup coarsely chopped celery
¼ cup olive oil
2 cups beef stock, fresh or canned
1 tablespoon arrowroot
2 tablespoons dry Marsala
Salt
Freshly ground black pepper

1. Combine 1 cup of Marsala, ¼ cup of olive oil, the lemon juice and bay leaves in a large glass or stainless-steel bowl.

2. Turn the fresh ham in this marinade until it is thoroughly moistened. Marinate at room temperature for at least 6 hours or in the refrigerator for at least 12 hours – turning the ham 2 or 3 times.

3. Preheat the oven to 350°.

4. Remove the ham from the marinade and pat it dry with paper towels.

5. Strain the marinade into a small bowl.

6. Combine the onions, carrots and celery and chop them together into very small pieces. (This chopped mixture is called a *battuto*, which is called a *soffritto* after it is cooked.)

7. Heat 2 tablespoons of olive oil in a heavy 4- to 6-quart flameproof casserole just large enough to hold the ham comfortably.

8. Add the *battuto* and cook over moderate heat, stirring frequently, for about 10 minutes, or until it is lightly colored.

9. Heat the remaining 2 tablespoons of oil in a heavy 10- to 12-inch skillet until a light haze forms over the oil.

10. Brown the ham in the skillet, starting it fat side down and turning it with 2 wooden spoons. When it is a golden-brown color all over, place the ham on top of the *soffritto* in the casserole and insert a meat thermometer deep into the thickest part of the meat.

11. Discard almost all of the fat from the skillet, leaving just a film on the bottom.

12. Pour in the strained marinade and boil it briskly over high heat, stirring and scraping in any browned bits that cling to the pan.

13. When the marinade has reduced to about half its original quantity, add it to the casserole along with the beef stock. If the liquid does not come ⅓ of the way up the side of the ham, add more stock.

14. Bring the casserole to a boil on top of the stove, cover and place on the middle shelf of the oven.

15. Braise the ham until the thermometer reaches 185° – which should take 3 to 3½ hours.

16. Transfer the ham to a heated platter, and let it rest for about 15 minutes to make carving easier.

17. Strain the sauce from the casserole through a fine sieve into a 1½- to 2-quart saucepan, pressing down hard on the vegetables to extract all their juices before discarding them.

18. Skim the surface of fat, then bring the sauce to a simmer over moderate heat.

19. Mix the arrowroot with 2 additional tablespoons of Marsala and, when the arrowroot has dissolved, stir it into the simmering sauce.

20. Continue cooking, stirring constantly, until the sauce thickens and clears. Do not let it boil. Taste the sauce for seasoning.

21. Carve the ham into thin slices and arrange the slices in a row on a heated serving platter.

22. Pour a few tablespoons of the sauce over the ham before serving it, and pass the rest separately.

Ham Braised in Burgundy

Schinken in Burgunder   *To serve 6 to 8*

**Half a precooked smoked ham, butt or
  shank end, about 5 to 6 pounds
2 cups water
2 cups red Burgundy or other dry red wine
1 medium-sized onion, peeled and thinly
  sliced
1 medium-sized tomato, peeled, seeded
  and coarsely chopped
1 whole clove, crushed with a mortar and
  pestle
1 small bay leaf
1 tablespoon butter, softened
1 tablespoon flour**

1. Preheat the oven to 350°.
2. With a small, sharp knife, separate the rind
from the ham and place the rind in a 1- to
2-quart saucepan.
3. Trim the ham of all but a ¼-inch layer of
fat.
4. Pour 2 cups of water over the rind, bring
to a boil over high heat, then reduce the heat
to low and simmer uncovered for 20 minutes.
5. Strain the liquid through a sieve into a bowl
and discard the rind.
6. Pour 1 cup of the rind stock into a shallow
roasting pan just large enough to hold the
ham comfortably.

7. Add 1 cup of the wine, and the onion,
tomato, clove and bay leaf.
8. Place the ham, fat side up, in the pan and
bake uncovered in the middle of the oven for
about 1 hour.
9. Baste the ham thoroughly every 20
minutes with the pan liquid. The ham is done
when it can easily be pierced with a fork.
10. Transfer the ham to a heated platter and
let it rest for easier carving while you prepare
the sauce.
11. Skim and discard all the fat from the pan
liquid and stir in the remaining 1 cup of wine.
12. Bring to a boil over high heat, meanwhile
scraping in any brown bits clinging to the bottom or sides of the pan, and boil briskly for
a minute or two.
13. In a small bowl, make a paste of the butter and flour, and stir it bit by bit into the pan.
14. Cook over low heat, stirring constantly,
for 5 minutes, or until the sauce is smooth
and slightly thickened.
15. Strain it through a fine sieve into a small
saucepan and taste for seasoning.
16. To serve, carve the ham into ¼-inch
slices and arrange the slices attractively, in
overlapping layers, on a large heated platter.
17. Moisten the slices with a few spoonfuls
of the Burgundy sauce, and serve the remaining sauce separately in a sauceboat.

Pork-Stuffed Cabbage Rolls

Töltött Káposzta   *To serve 4 to 6*

CABBAGE ROLLS

2 pounds sauerkraut, fresh, canned or packaged
1 large head green cabbage (2 to 3 pounds)
2 tablespoons lard or bacon fat
1 cup finely chopped onions
¼ teaspoon finely chopped garlic
1 pound ground lean pork
¼ cup rice, cooked in boiling salted water (¾ cup cooked)
2 lightly beaten eggs
2 tablespoons sweet Hungarian paprika
⅛ teaspoon marjoram
1 teaspoon salt
Freshly ground black pepper
1 cup water mixed with 1 cup tomato purée

1. Wash the sauerkraut in cold water, then soak in cold water 10 to 20 minutes to reduce sourness. Squeeze dry and set aside.

2. In a large saucepan, bring to a boil enough salted water to cover the cabbage.

3. Add the cabbage, turn the heat to low and simmer 8 minutes.

4. Remove the cabbage and let it drain while it cools enough to handle. Pull off the large unbroken leaves and lay them on paper towels to drain and cool further.

5. In a 10-inch skillet, heat the lard or bacon fat on high heat until a light haze forms over it.

6. Add the onions and garlic and cook them, stirring occasionally, until lightly colored.

7. In a mixing bowl, combine the pork, rice, eggs, paprika, marjoram, the onion-garlic mixture, salt and a few grindings of black pepper. Mix well with a fork or wooden spoon.

8. Place 2 tablespoons of the stuffing in the center of one of the wilted cabbage leaves and, beginning with the thick end of one leaf, fold over the sides, then roll the whole leaf tightly, as you would a small bundle. Repeat with more leaves until all the stuffing has been used.

9. Spread the sauerkraut on the bottom of

1. Put a mixture of pork, rice, eggs and paprika on blanched cabbage leaves.

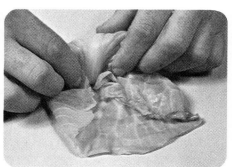

2. Fold each leaf over from the sides and start rolling from the root end.

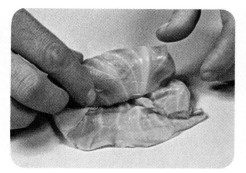

3. Roll the leaves tightly, carefully tucking in the sides as you go.

4. The pork-stuffed cabbage roll is now shown in its completed form.

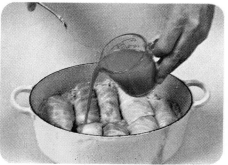

5. Place cabbage rolls on sauerkraut, add water, tomato purée and simmer.

6. Serve the stuffed cabbage rolls with their own sauce, and sauerkraut.

a 5-quart casserole and arrange the cabbage rolls on top of it. Add the water mixed with the tomato purée. Bring the liquid to a boil, then cover the pan tightly and cook the stuffed cabbage over low heat for 1 hour.
10. Transfer the rolls from the casserole to a warm platter.

SAUCE
3 tablespoons unsalted butter
2 tablespoons flour
1 cup sour cream

1. In a small saucepan on medium heat, melt the butter and stir in the flour. Continue to stir until the flour browns slightly.
2. Gradually stir in the cream, continuing to stir until the sauce is thick and smooth.
3. Stir the sauce into the sauerkraut and simmer 5 to 10 minutes longer.
4. With a fork or slotted spoon, lift the sauerkraut onto a serving platter. Arrange the cabbage rolls on the sauerkraut and pour some of the sauce over them.
5. Serve the rest of the sauce in a sauceboat.

Pork and Ham Balls

To make 32 meatballs

1 cup fresh bread crumbs
3 tablespoons milk
1 pound fresh lean pork, finely ground, combined with ½ pound cooked smoked ham, finely ground
1 tablespoon prepared mustard
1 tablespoon finely chopped fresh parsley
1 egg, lightly beaten

Freshly ground black pepper
2 tablespoons butter
2 tablespoons vegetable oil
¾ cup dry red wine

1. Soak the bread crumbs in the milk for about 5 minutes, then combine them with the ground pork and ham in a large mixing bowl.
2. Add the mustard, parsley, lightly beaten egg and a few grindings of black pepper, and with a large spoon mix them thoroughly together.
3. Form the mixture into small balls about 1 inch in diameter and chill for at least ½ hour.
4. Preheat the oven to 350°.
5. Over high heat, melt the butter with the oil in a large, heavy skillet. When the foam subsides, add the ham balls. To help keep their shape as they brown, roll the balls around in the hot fat by shaking the pan back and forth over the burner.
6. When the ham balls are well browned on all sides (this should take about 5 minutes), transfer them with a slotted spoon to a 2-quart casserole.
7. Pour off all but a thin film of fat from the skillet and pour in the wine. Bring it to a boil over high heat, scraping and stirring into it any brown bits clinging to the bottom and sides of the pan.
8. Cook briskly for about a minute, then pour the wine into the casserole.
9. Cover tightly and bake in the middle of the oven for about 30 minutes, basting the ham balls after 15 minutes with the wine.
10. Serve either directly from the casserole or arrange the balls on a heated platter and pour the sauce over them.

Well-seasoned pork rolled into balls forms the basis for the prickly looking "pearl balls" shown above arranged in the rack of a Chinese steamer.

Pearl Balls

Chen-chu-jou-wan   *To serve 4*

½ cup glutinous rice
4 dried Chinese mushrooms, 1 to 1½ inches in diameter
1 pound lean boneless pork, finely ground
1 egg, lightly beaten

1 tablespoon soy sauce
1½ teaspoons salt
½ teaspoon sugar
1 teaspoon finely chopped, peeled fresh ginger root
6 canned water chestnuts, drained and finely chopped
1 scallion, including the green top, finely chopped

PREPARE AHEAD: 1. In a small bowl, cover the rice with 1 cup of cold water and soak for 2 hours. Then drain the rice through a sieve, spread it out on a cloth towel and let it dry.

2. In a small bowl, cover the mushrooms with ½ cup of warm water and let them soak for 30 minutes. Discard the water. With a cleaver or knife, cut away and discard the mushroom stems, and chop the caps fine.

3. Combine the pork, egg, soy sauce, salt and sugar in a mixing bowl. With your fingers or a large spoon, mix together until the ingredients are thoroughly blended. Then add the ginger, chopped mushrooms, water chestnuts and scallions, and mix thoroughly again. Scoop up about 2 tablespoons of the mixture and, with your hands, shape it into a ball 1 inch in diameter. Repeat this process with the remaining pork mixture, moistening your hands from time to time with a little cold water. Arrange the balls side by side on a strip of wax paper.

4. Roll one pork ball at a time in the rice, pressing down gently but firmly as you roll so that the rice grains adhere to the meat. Set the rice-coated balls back on wax paper.

TO COOK: 1. Pour enough boiling water into the lower part of a steamer to come within an inch of the cooking rack.

2. Choose a heatproof plate about ½ inch smaller in diameter than the pot so that the steam can rise and circulate around the pork balls as they steam. Arrange the pork balls on it.

3. Place the plate on the rack, bring the water in the steamer to a boil, and cover the pan tightly. Keeping the water at a continuous boil and replenishing it if it boils away, steam the pork balls for 30 minutes.

4. Set the steaming plate on a large platter and serve at once.

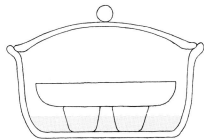

This cutaway view shows the construction of an improvised steamer: A plate is set, two inches above water, on two small, heatproof dishes set right side up in a large, tightly covered roasting pan. There must be enough space around the edge of the plate to allow the steam to rise and circulate freely.

Pearl balls, shaped from a ground pork and water chestnut mixture, are rolled in rice until well coated. Arrange them for cooking in an aluminum steamer, set well apart on paper toweling to prevent the balls from sticking together.

English Pork Pie

To serve 6 to 8

PASTRY
2 cups flour
1 teaspoon salt
1 teaspoon baking powder
1½ sticks butter (¼ pound each)
1 egg yolk
¼ cup ice water
FILLING
1 pound sausage meat
½ pound cooked ham, cut in strips
¼ pound tongue, cut in strips
2 hard-cooked eggs
ASPIC
3½ cups cold clear stock
1 tablespoon tomato paste
5 tablespoons gelatin
¼ cup sherry
3 egg whites, stiffly beaten

PASTRY: 1. Sift the flour, salt and baking powder together on a pastry board or marble slab.
2. Make a well in the center and in it put the butter, egg yolk and ice water.
3. Work the center ingredients to a smooth paste, then work in the flour with the heel of your hand.
4. Wrap the dough in wax paper and chill in the refrigerator for 1 to 2 hours.
5. Roll out half the pastry about ¼ inch thick and line a raised pie mold with it.
6. Place ⅙ of the sausage in a layer on the bottom.
7. Cover it with half the ham, another layer of sausage, the tongue, more sausage, the sliced eggs, sausage, the rest of the ham and a final layer of sausage.
8. Brush the edge of the dough with beaten egg.
9. Roll the rest of the dough a little thicker than the bottom crust.
10. Cover the top and trim the edges neatly.
11. Make a small hole in the center and cover it with a flower made with small rounds of pastry. Brush the top with beaten egg.

12. Chill in the refrigerator for at least an hour.
13. Preheat the oven to 350°.
14. Bake the pie for about an hour, or until it is golden brown.
15. Remove from the oven and allow to cool.
ASPIC: 16. In deep saucepan put the stock, tomato paste, gelatin, sherry and beaten egg whites.
17. Beat with a large wire whisk over a slow fire until the mixture just comes to a boil.
18. Strain through a damp cloth that has been placed over a large strainer.
19. Reserve one cup of aspic for the pie, place the rest in 2 shallow cake tins and put in the refrigerator to set.
20. When the pie is cool, take the reserved cup of aspic and stir it over ice until it is on the point of setting.
21. Take the center flower off the pie and pour the aspic into the hole. Replace the flower, and chill in the refrigerator for 2 to 3 hours before serving.
22. When ready, carefully unmold the pie and place it on a serving dish, garnished with chopped set aspic.

Tortillas with Pig's Feet

Tostadas Estilo Guadalajara   *To serve 6*

SAUCE
6 medium tomatoes, peeled, seeded and
**   finely chopped**
1 cup finely chopped onions
2 teaspoons dried oregano
½ teaspoon finely chopped garlic
½ cup red wine vinegar
1 teaspoon sugar
1 teaspoon salt

4 cups *frijoles refritos* (*below*)
5 tablespoons olive oil or vegetable oil
2 tablespoons red wine vinegar
¼ teaspoon salt
3 cups finely shredded iceberg lettuce
⅓ cup lard
12 tortillas
2 or 3 pickled pig's feet, boned and coarsely chopped
1 cup coarsely chopped onions
½ cup freshly grated Parmesan cheese
4 canned *jalapeño* chilies, rinsed in cold water and cut lengthwise into ⅛-inch strips

1. Combine the tomatoes, 1 cup of finely chopped onions, oregano, garlic, vinegar, sugar and salt for the sauce in a bowl and, with a large spoon, mix them together thoroughly.
2. Set the sauce aside.
3. For the topping, prepare the *frijoles refritos*, cover them and keep them warm over the lowest possible heat.
4. In a large bowl, beat the oil, vinegar and salt together until they are thoroughly combined.
5. Drop in the lettuce and toss lightly with a spoon until it is coated evenly with the dressing.
6. In a heavy 8- to 10-inch skillet, melt 2 tablespoons of the lard over moderate heat until a light haze forms above it.
7. One at a time, fry the tortillas for 1 minute on each side, or until they are light gold. Drain on a double thickness of paper towels. As you proceed, replenish the lard in the pan, 1 tablespoon at a time, when necessary.
8. Assemble the *tostadas* in the following fashion: Place 2 tortillas side by side on each serving plate.
9. Spread about ⅓ cup of the refried beans on the surface of each tortilla, scatter ¼ cup of lettuce on the beans, then top with layers of pig's feet, coarsely chopped onions and finally the sauce.

10. Sprinkle each *tostada* which 2 teaspoons of grated cheese and garnish with a few strips of *jalapeño* chili.

FRIJOLES REFRITOS
2 cups dried pink beans or dried red kidney beans
6 cups cold water
1 cup coarsely chopped onions
2 medium tomatoes, peeled, seeded and coarsely chopped, or substitute ⅔ cup chopped, drained, canned Italian plum tomatoes
½ teaspoon finely chopped garlic
1 teaspoon crumbled and seeded dried *pequín* chili
¼ teaspoon crumbled *epazote*, if available
¼ teaspoon freshly ground black pepper
½ cup lard
1 teaspoon salt

NOTE: Wear rubber gloves when handling the hot chilies.
1. Place the beans in a colander or sieve and run cold water over them until the draining water runs clear.
2. Pick out and discard any black or shriveled beans.
3. In a 3-quart heavy pot, combine the water, ½ cup of the onions, ¼ cup of the tomatoes, ¼ teaspoon of the garlic, the chili, *epazote* (if used) and pepper, and drop in the beans. Bring the water to a boil over high heat, then half-cover the pan and reduce the heat to low.
4. Simmer the beans for about 15 minutes and stir in 1 tablespoon of the lard.
5. Simmer, half covered, for 1½ hours, add the teaspoon of salt, and over the lowest possible heat, simmer for another 30 minutes, or until the beans are very tender and have absorbed all their cooking liquid. During the last half hour of cooking, stir the beans gently now and then to prevent their sticking to the bottom of the pan.
6. Remove the pan from the heat, and cover

it to keep the beans warm.

7. In a heavy 12-inch skillet, melt 2 more tablespoons of the lard over moderate heat until a light haze forms above it.

8. Add the remaining chopped onions and garlic, turn the heat down to moderate, and fry for about 5 minutes, or until the onions are transparent but not brown.

9. Stir in the remaining tomatoes and simmer for 2 or 3 minutes.

10. Fry the cooked beans in the following fashion: Add 3 tablespoons of the beans to the pan of simmering sauce, mash them with a fork, then stir in 1 tablespoon of the remaining lard.

11. Continue adding and mashing the beans in similar amounts, following each addition with another tablespoon of lard until all the beans and lard have been used.

12. Cook over low heat for 10 minutes, stirring frequently, until the beans are fairly dry.

1. Cut the beef, pork and pork fat into small cubes and mix them well with the salt, pepper, coriander and vinegar.

2. Let the meat stand in the marinade at room temperature for at least 3 hours, turning it over several times. Then grind the meat through the medium blade of a food grinder.

3. If you have a sausage stuffer attachment for the grinder, cut the sausage casing into 1-yard lengths and tie one end securely with thread. Put the meat mixture through the grinder again, stuffing it into the casing. Twist the casing at 2- or 3-inch intervals to make individual sausages.

4. If you don't have a sausage stuffer, grind the meat again, form it into sausage shapes, then roll them lightly in flour.

5. In either case refrigerate the sausages overnight.

6. Broil either over charcoal or in the broiler about 20 minutes, or until they are well done. Turn them often to brown all sides and to cook evenly.

Spiced Beef and Pork Sausages

To serve 10 to 12

3 pounds sirloin steak
2 pounds boneless pork
¼ pound pork fat
4 teaspoons salt
2 teaspoons black pepper
3 tablespoons crushed coriander
¼ cup vinegar
4 yards sausage casing (optional)
Flour (optional)

Danish Meat Patties

Frikadeller   *Makes 8 to 10 patties*

½ pound boneless veal
½ pound boneless pork
1 medium onion, coarsely chopped or
  grated (½ cup)
3 tablespoons flour
1½ cups club soda
1 egg, well beaten
1 teaspoon salt
¼ teaspoon pepper
4 tablespoons butter
2 tablespoons vegetable oil

1. Put the veal, pork and chopped onion twice through the finest blade of a meat

grinder, or have the butcher grind the meats together and then grate in the onion yourself.

2. In a large mixing bowl, vigorously beat the flour into the ground meat mixture with a wooden spoon, or use an electric mixer equipped with a pastry arm or paddle.

3. Gradually beat in the club soda, a few tablespoons at a time, and continue to beat until the meat is light and fluffy.

4. Now thoroughly beat in the egg, salt and pepper.

5. Cover the bowl with aluminum foil or plastic wrap and refrigerate for 1 hour; this will make the meat mixture firmer and easier to handle.

6. Shape the mixture into oblongs about 4 inches long, 2 inches wide and 1 inch thick. Melt the butter and oil over high heat in a heavy 10- to 12-inch skillet.

7. When the foam subsides, lower the heat to moderate and add the meat patties, 4 or 5 at a time, taking care not to crowd them.

8. Cook about 6 to 8 minutes on each side, turning the patties with a wide spatula or two wooden spoons. When they are a rich mahogany brown, remove them from the pan and set them aside on a heated platter.

9. Continue with the remaining patties. Because *frikadeller* contain pork, they should never be served rare. To be certain they are cooked through, puncture one with the tip of a small knife. The juices should run clear and show no tinge of pink.

10. *Frikadeller* are traditionally accompanied by boiled potatoes and pickled beets, cucumber salad or red cabbage.

Made of ground veal and pork mixed with onions and an egg, these patties are fried in butter until both sides turn brown and are almost crusty.

INDEX